FROM NAM TO NORMAL

Battle of the Demons

Richard A Price

ISBN-13: 9781495356186
ISBN-10: 1495356183
Library of Congress Control Number: 2014901795
CreateSpace Independent Publishing Platform
North Charleston, South Carolina

Dedication

This book is dedicated to my Vietnam buddy, my first fire team leader, and my best friend and brother, Gary Ward Grimshaw, who was born in Gouverneur, New York, on May 5, 1943, and passed away on January 20, 2012. I was blessed to have a man like Gary be part of my life for forty-six of his sixty-eight years.

Our journey of forty-six years of brotherhood started in Port Hueneme, California, in the spring of 1966. We met when we were assigned to Mobile Construction Battalion Eight, US Navy Seabees. I had come from a Seabees boot camp in Davisville, Rhode Island; and Gary had come from navy boot camp in Great Lakes, Illinois. We were both engineering aides (EAs) and were assigned to the Engineering Platoon, Headquarters Company.

Most EAs had a background in the outdoors, and a common topic of discussion was the hunting of various species of wild game. Gary and I took the topic beyond talk and investigated what we could hunt in Southern California. We had seen valley quail while on specialized survey training in the foothills surrounding Oxnard, California. We decided that quail would become our prey of the day. Little did I realize then that the love for hunting would be the initial bond that would develop into a brotherhood lasting more than four decades. Our two tours in Vietnam together also contributed to our tight bond. We were in the same squad for both of our tours. The only time we were apart was when one of us was on detached duty from battalion or on different jobsites.

After our separation from active duty, we remained close friends. Our friendship became stronger and stronger as the years passed. Our trust in each other was enhanced as we shared the challenges and heartaches of our similar demons. We cried on each other's shoulders, drowned a number of our demons in alcohol, and justified each other's lot in life. Over the years we introduced each other to our various loves in the outdoors. Gary introduced me to turkey-and-waterfowl hunting; I introduced him to walleye fishing and muzzle-loader and crossbow hunting for white-tailed deer in Ohio.

Our brotherhood wasn't isolated just to hunting and fishing. We were always there for each other. I must say that I called in many more markers than he did. It didn't matter to Gary; he didn't keep score. If you were his friend, you could count on him as surely as day followed night. He was always there if I needed him and would hang in there with me until the need existed no more.

Unfortunately, we also shared another common bond—post-traumatic stress disorder (PTSD).

Upon our return from Vietnam, neither Gary nor I realized we suffered from PTSD. We had become so close that we were actually enablers for each other. We could trust that we would always support each other with our actions. We justified our divorces, overindulged in alcohol, resented the establishment, and were reluctant to trust no more than very few people.

Thank you, God, for making a place in heaven for my brother, Gary. A place inhabited by angels, not demons. A place where love replaces the need for trust. A place where peace and happiness eliminate the need for hypervigilance. A place without intrusive thoughts, nightmares, or flashbacks. A place where he can rest throughout eternity, reaping the benefits he earned in this life by being a man dedicated to his values, integrity, ethics, duty, and loyalty to a friend.

God bless you, brother.

Table of Contents

Author's Note

Don't skip this section—it's the key to understanding this book. Without understanding my intentions, you might think this is merely a story about my life during Vietnam and the forty-four years that followed my service there. That's not it at all.

My one and only purpose for writing this book is to provide a tool for other Vietnam veterans to use in examining their lives. Many articles, stories, and texts will address everything contained in this book concerning PTSD. However, these various writings tend to fragment PTSD by dwelling on a single aspect or simply looking at a list of symptoms. When PTSD is oversimplified, many veterans are led to believe in a quick fix or even a cure. When that cure isn't attained, however, the veteran may give up without knowing how long and how difficult the journey home from PTSD actually is. Those of us who suffer from PTSD seek nothing more than to minimize its debilitating effects on our lives. When we begin to struggle with these effects, we realize how deep and broad PTSD actually is.

Vietnam veterans, for the most part, have trust in their brothers. It's this trust I'm relying on to validate my goal for writing this book. If my story helps just one veteran find the peace I've found in identifying and confronting my PTSD demons, the effort has been worth it.

I may deviate from what is considered the proper way to present written material. I'm not concerned about being proper. My purpose is to give my Vietnam brothers a manual they can relate to while on their journey home from PTSD.

The sections written in the first-person voice are my personal experiences. Other sections are written as though I'm writing about you, a Vietnam veteran, in general. They are! For some sections or topics to have meaning, I had to look at the collective experiences of many veterans. All the observations and recommendations I share with you are those I have *personally* experienced or observed. They are my perceptions and are related to you as I interpreted them.

I have repeated myself when discussing various emotions, reactions, and situations. There is a reason for this! A veteran may not recognize a symptom when given a conceptual example or scant details of the symptom or event. When re-acting or overreacting to a PTSD trigger, we tend to view it as a "black or white" moment. Without some repetition, the particular point I'm trying to make might be missed entirely. I repeat defining words such as *triggers, guilt, depression,* and *control* when I discuss our feelings, emotions, reactions, and situations. These are not mere words to the Vietnam veteran suffering from PTSD—they are his life. By approaching PTSD in this way, I pray that this book will become an instrument for other Vietnam veterans to use in battling their demons.

This is not an "I know it all" book. I'm not a psychiatrist, psychologist, therapist, or social worker. I'm a Vietnam veteran who suffers from PTSD, which I didn't identify for many years and which has taken me another ten years to find tools to deal with my symptoms. The results have paid off! I hope this book will be one of the tools you can use to find peace and happiness while living with PTSD. Don't kid yourself; the journey isn't easy. But what has ever been easy for the Vietnam veteran?

God bless you, brother, and may God look after you and your family on your journey home.

CHAPTER ONE

Operation Normal:
My Goals and Dreams, 1968

"**I** just want to be normal." This is the statement
I said to myself during my return trip home
after my second tour in Vietnam. Normal, as I had
known it, existed only as a vision in the distant
past. Nearly two years in Vietnam had taught me
a different kind of normal, a normal accelerated
by an adrenaline rush to be accepted by a society I
had left behind. I assumed that veterans of any war
experienced the same feelings. I was soon to learn
that wasn't the case. Vietnam veterans came home
to face the demons of combat as well as demons on
the home front.

I was an engineering aide in the US Navy
Seabees (the engineering component of the
US Marine Corps). My first tour was in Chu Lai,
Vietnam (1966–1967). We were the Engineering
Platoon of Headquarters Company, Seabee
Battalion, Mobile Construction Battalion (MCB)

Eight. As an E-4, my battalion job was to be a drafts-man and surveyor. My military responsibility was to be an M60 machine gunner and eventually the fire team leader. The Engineering Platoon (First Platoon) was the reinforced weapons platoon for the company. The platoon consisted of a mortar squad, a 3.5 rocket launcher squad, and an M60 machine gun squad. Each squad had three fire teams with a specialized heavy weapon in each team. During my second tour I was squad leader of the M60 machine gun squad. While in Chu Lai, my battalion spent the majority of its time on job assignments. We were subject to some mortar at-tacks and mines on Route One as well as sniper fire and booby traps while working on projects and surveying jobs.

It was in Chu Lai that I extended my enlistment for a year for the promotion to E-5. That extension would enable me to be an instructor in NAVSCON (Naval Schools Construction). Since junior high school, I had always wanted to become a teacher, and I felt this pursuit would give me an opportu-nity to test the waters.

I must admit that I had other self-serving rea-sons for becoming an E-5. To begin with, it got me out of the field and back to base camp to take the exam. It would allow me entrance into the Non-Commissioned Officers (NCO) club, enable me to draw commuter rations, and live off base once I was back in Port Hueneme. Little did I realize that the extension for E-5 would buy me a ticket on the big bird back to Nam. I should have realized this would happen, since I had to extend for a year to receive the rate.

I came home on advanced party with a small number of other men from my battalion. The C-130 took off from the Chu Lai Airfield at night, while a firefight took place on the outer perimeter. I cut my thirty-day leave short by almost three weeks after a heated confrontation with my father, who was justified in not being happy with me. I returned to Port Hueneme and worked on deployment-completion reports until I started my instructor training course.

After the main body returned from their leave, a number of new NCOs, including me, were sent to squad leader training school. Prior to our NAVSCON training, the entire battalion had four weeks of military training, the majority of which was spent at Camp Pendleton. With my military training as well as squad leader and instructor training schools completed, I was assigned to NAVSCON and given one week to prepare my surveying lessons.

On the Friday afternoon before I was to start teaching on Monday, I was given orders for my second tour in Vietnam. I was detached to the Third Marine Shore Party. This tour started in the fall of 1967. Upon our arrival at the Gia Le combat base, located between Phu Bai and Hue City, some others and I, who were on the advanced detachment, joined the remaining element of Headquarters

3

and Supply Company, Third Marine Division, Third Shore Party. The skeleton group of marines included a reinforced company of the Third Shore Party, two 155mm howitzers, and an antose, a tank-type vehicle, which mounted six recoilless rifles.

Upon my arrival, I was assigned the job of taking sounding shots of the Perfume River. To a surveyor this is a relatively easy job. I would take my crew of three marines to the Ramp in Hue, load my equipment and crew into a jon-boat, and head west and south along the river in Hue. We would set up and take sounding shots (with a transit, not a rifle) every fifty feet along the Perfume River. Back in base camp, I reduced the day's field notes to cross sections of the river. The purpose of this job was to provide navigation charts of the Perfume River through Hue City. The job continued until the day before the 1968 Tet Offensive.

Tet started during the early morning hours of January 31, 1968. That same day the first flight of the main body of the battalion arrived. My MCB Eight squad was on that flight. At that time my surveying job ended, and my military duties became top priority. As an E-5 my military role was squad leader of an M60 machine gun squad. No additional flights could make it in for several days, so my squad filed in alongside the Third Shore Party Marines, who were defending the Gia Le perimeter.

With the exception of constructing a temporary bridge across the Perfume River to replace the original bridge, which had been destroyed during the early hours of the offensive, I spent the majority of the next twenty-two days with my squad and marines, defending our perimeter. Hugging the dirt during 122mm rocket attacks and firefights along our perimeter was the main order of business. Following Tet, we rebuilt our camp and started projects again. It seemed like we had just become comfortable, as comfortable as one could become in Vietnam, when the second spring offensive started. Once again we were on the perimeter, ducking rockets and mortars. The 101st Airborne's Camp Eagle was now located to the west of our perimeter, limiting but not eliminating the amount of ground action on my squad's section of the wire.

As this offensive wound down, I drew near my separation from active duty. During Tet I had acquired a Chinese RPD machine gun. The machine gun had caught the eye of a battalion personnel man who wanted it in the worst way. He told me, "If you give me the machine gun, I'll cut your orders back to the world thirty days early." Since I knew I couldn't take the gun back home anyway, I took him up on his offer. A close friend of mine, John, also got his orders cut. A couple of days later, we turned our weapons into the armory and checked out of battalion with our orders in hand.

Now what? We had our orders but no way to get from the Gia Le combat base to Da Nang and ultimately White Elephant, our "travel-agency" to get home. John suggested we go to the 101st and see if we could hop on a chopper heading to Da Nang. Following Tet and in preparation for the Battle of the A Shau Valley, the 101st Airborne Division had relocated just west of our perimeter. We walked to the chopper pad, and, fortunately for us, a chopper was heading to Da Nang. The pilot asked if either of us was checked out on the M60s. He needed a gunner. Manning the gun was how I paid for my ticket to Da Nang. Thank God, there were no incidents on the way. We arrived in Da Nang and found our way to White Elephant to check in. Needless to say, here came another zinger. Back in Hue the personnel man sat with my machine gun and forgot to tell us we wouldn't be on a manifest back to the States for thirty days. What in the hell were we to do for thirty days in Nam without weapons or a place to stay? A good friend from my hometown was in Mobile Construction Battalion Fifty-Three, located between Marble and Monkey Mountain, in Da Nang. I thought," If we can find him, we can at least hide in Camp Haskins for thirty days. "John and I finally located Ted's battalion, and he informed us that we could" get a hop" on a cargo flight going to Conus (military slang for the continental United States). He secured a weapons carrier and promptly delivered us to the 15th Aeroport. After signing up, we had only a four-hour wait before boarding the big bird home.

This big bird was a casket flight. We sat on the floor, leaning against the aluminum boxes

6

that held the bodies of our fallen brothers. For nearly thirty-six hours, I rested against the casket of Marine LCPL Shannon. While we had no conversation, my thoughts and questions about him burned in my mind. In-country you didn't have time to think that deeply. I could only guess that once I was heading home, I could let my guard down and think like a real person. In Vietnam the only real things I could relate to were my buddies. When we landed at Travis Air Force Base outside of San Francisco, I vowed never to get on an aircraft for the rest of my life. Isn't that a great way to start becoming normal?

John and I were bused to Treasure Island Naval Station and directed to the marine-transit barracks. Within ten minutes, I almost wished I was back in-country. It was dark when we got to the barracks, so John and I took racks by the lighted hallway. We watched cockroaches dart across the floor, and bedbugs bit us all night.

Waking early from an exhausting sleep, we dug through our seabags to retrieve our dress blues, which were mandatory for us to get off base. In general, wearing uniforms off base wasn't recommended and was frequently prohibited. Since we had no civilian clothes, I guess we left the navy with few options. This was one of the few times I experienced being allowed to wear uniforms off base. You can only imagine what they looked and smelled like after they spent nearly a year in a seabag in the lovely Vietnam climate.

John and I caught a bus to San Francisco to buy some civilian clothes, then went to the bus station for a quick change and finally to the cleaners to get our uniforms cleaned and made presentable. Tired from these exhausting activities, we decided to hit as many topless bars as possible before heading back to Treasure Island. I was the appointed counter, and we made it to fifteen before heading back. Monday through Thursday, I was assigned shore patrol duty at a movie theater and was processed out on Friday.

Processing out at Treasure Island was very efficient. Making me a civilian again took approximately two hours. The experience I remember most—and one that affects me to this day—was my exiting physical. The group I was part of numbered between six and eight men. We went before the doctor in a line similar to the shot line in boot camp. As we paraded before him, fully clothed, he asked several questions, signed our papers, and released us to move on. Before he signed my papers, I asked him about the wound and pain in my left knee. I had taken shrapnel in my knee several days before leaving Nam. My injury wasn't bad enough to take me out of the field. Our corpsman wrapped my knee, and I continued to function. The doctor's response was, "I can send you to the hospital here, or you can go to a veterans hospital when you get home." I assume most Vietnam veterans would have made the same decision I did. I had to get out of that place, so I took my separation papers and ran!

With my packet of papers in hand, I made it to the bus station and bought a ticket to Long Beach. My aunt lived there with my cousin Jerry, a retired senior chief who had enlisted at age seventeen during the Second World War. His ship, the USS *Thompson*, hit mines twice during the Korean War, and after serving in the Vietnam theater, he finally retired. My single cousin spent most of his time in a couple of local bars and in the Long Beach Chiefs Club. This felt like the perfect place to hide until I could figure out just what it would take to begin my normal life.

During this period I totally lost track of time, and after a number of weeks, my aunt, whom my parents were pressuring, suggested I should go back home. I really didn't want to go home with the many mixed-up feelings I was having. My mind wasn't clear, nor was the direction I wanted to take. Long Beach became my comfort zone. In addition to that, my cousin was the surrogate buddy I had left in Vietnam. I was in turmoil as to what to do.

At this point I fell back on my engineering mind-set and on paper jotted down how I should act and what it would take for me to be the person society expected me to be. Funny—no one had pressured me to be anything. These decisions were mine, and I had contrived them alone. Many of these decisions and battlefield promises were burned into my mind during the many hours I had to think while in-country. My list was short but very long term, and it would involve the lives of many people. It included getting married, having children, securing a decent job, and possibly going to college to be a teacher.

While I was in Vietnam, I had been writing to two girls, one from Oregon and one from Texas. Both seemed like really nice girls, and I could imagine becoming involved with either one. There's no doubt in my mind that in my subconscious I was looking for a wife. Not having met either girl in person, I decided to flip a coin to determine whether I would go back to Ohio by the northern or southern route. Texas won, and the next day I left California for Lake Jackson, Texas. When arriving, I stayed with the parents of the girl's family who had introduced me to my Texas pen pal. I stayed there for nearly a month, getting acquainted with her. Before leaving for Ohio, I suggested that we consider marriage. We phoned each other almost daily, and within a two-week period, she accepted my proposal to get married.

I was so proud of myself! I had gotten on the fast track to becoming normal. I was always very independent and a little stubborn, and my squad leader duties in the Nam had strengthened both of these characteristics. My parents were so happy that I was finally home that they didn't oppose my decision. I don't think it would have made much difference anyway. Consequently, soon after she arrived in Ohio, we became husband and wife.

My net worth at the time was a 1963 Dodge pickup truck I had purchased between deployments. It was a California truck, and it had no heater. After borrowing $450 to buy some furniture, we set up our household in a one-bedroom apartment in Newark, Ohio. I went back to my old place of employment, a large telephone company in Columbus.

This may sound like a simple thing, but as with many things Vietnam veterans came home to, life wasn't easy. My department had been relocated to a new site, and they didn't want to give me the pay advances I should have received. For two months I fought them and refused to move to the new site. During that time I worked for a local surveying company and was a surveyor for the state of Ohio (Ohio Department of Transportation) and a draftsman for a glass company in Lancaster. Finally, my old company found a drafting job for me at the plant where I had previously worked. This job didn't include the raises. The company felt I should be grateful. In some respects I was, but at the same time I began harboring more negative feelings.

It was at this time that I noticed my anger escalating. During my first day on the job, the department coordinator was assigned to familiarize me with the drafting equipment I would be using. He had been a draftsman for nine months after completing a two-year tech school degree. I had nearly seven years of experience in drafting and surveying. Consequently, I told him to get the hell out of my face—I had forgotten more about drafting than he knew. These types of triggers, or events that bring about anxiety or anger, coupled with other negative experiences, only added to the anguish and disappointment I felt upon arriving back in the States.

My triggers had started when I couldn't wear my uniform and ribbons off base. I also became wary of even mentioning that I was a Vietnam veteran. I was never short of pride, and having to hide this fact made my blood boil. Nevertheless, I took the job and dedicated myself to it. I had joined a new department with new people. Within eight months I advanced to coordinator of the department.

My family was never known for its wealth, but we were rich in our values. We had a great work ethic, were trustworthy, showed respect to others (if it was deserved), and viewed duty as our most important value. There's nothing like a good Welsh upbringing to instill these characteristics in a person. Like so many Vietnam veterans, my work ethic and my need to be busy became problematic and led to my becoming a workaholic. I was blinded to the fact that performing this duty well could lead to many more problems in the future.

Within three months, my wife became pregnant with our first daughter. Talk about being on the fast track! I was elated and felt like my plan was all coming together. That winter I enrolled at The Ohio State University (OSU) in Newark. I felt like my goals were all in place. Now it was up to me to follow through and take them to completion.

I assured myself that if I achieved these goals, I would certainly be a normal person in society and be accepted by that society.

I dedicated myself both at work and in the classroom. In the spring of 1969, I was offered a teaching position in a local vocational school for the following school year. I would be teaching drafting and surveying. A degree wasn't necessary—only years of experience in the trade. I quit my job in June and attended a six-week workshop before beginning to teach. During this time I went to school during the day (8:30 a.m. to 3:30 p.m.) and worked the 6:00-p.m.-to-2:00-a.m. shift at an all-night gas station. I had worked until 2:00 a.m. on the day my first daughter was born. I was so exhausted that I had difficulty getting up to take my wife to the hospital.

I didn't recognize that I, like many other Vietnam veterans, was falling into the workaholic trap, which destroyed or severely damaged many families. In my way of thinking, no one could fault me for being so dedicated to reaching my goals. I was like a train engineer with no passengers on board—but I didn't know it yet. I felt good in my own world and believed I was on the right track. In retrospect there were many other things going on in my life and mind that I neither recognized nor understood. With this lack of knowledge, I couldn't possibly address the demons that would haunt me for the next thirty-plus years.

CHAPTER TWO
Ambush in Conus:
Welcome Home

Early in the 2000s, when I started to understand PTSD and my symptoms, a different perspective began to emerge. For the first time, I started to look at the other side of situations, for which I had taken offense for so many decades. To analyze them, I had to look deep within myself. With the help of my limited knowledge of psychology, I concluded that I was just craving acknowledgment, acceptance, and validation. I came to realize that I had set some of my own ambushes. I had made up my mind that I wouldn't surrender to a society that, for the most part, rejected the Vietnam veteran in a multitude of ways. When I wasn't rejected, I was given a wide berth or ignored.

I didn't realize how those actions by society were so devastating to me. Like most returning vets, I was very vulnerable. Things said or done that seemed minor to most people affected me deeply, and the effects sometimes lasted for years. Regardless of who had set the ambush, I felt like I had been hit from all sides. The worst thing was that these ambushes always seemed to hit me cold. In Vietnam the potential for ambush was always present. I just didn't expect it here.

Vietnam veterans were under the umbrella of the World War II vets. Many of them looked on us as losers. We had never achieved the victory they had, and like the rest of the civilian population, they thought of Vietnam as a dirty war fought by men with little character and few, if any, values. But war statistics point out that the Vietnam veteran had four times as much trigger time as the average veteran of World War II. I'm not sure if this fact didn't contribute to their rejection of us. A common way for people to feel better about themselves is to put others down. It's just possible that World War II veterans actually admired us but had difficulty saying so.

The American people could turn only to politicians and the media to get information about the war. Politicians couldn't be trusted, and the media had such disdain for the war that anything they said was slanted. Why shouldn't the public form its opinions based on what they saw and heard? How else was the public to learn what the Vietnam War was really like? For that matter, how could they learn what the Vietnam soldier was really like?

The society I had left was nothing like the society I returned to. I can somewhat understand.

Our country was sick of a war it didn't understand, and many people voiced their opinions openly by exercising their First Amendment rights to oppose the war. I couldn't understand a country that felt veterans of other wars were heroes but Vietnam veterans were the scum of the earth.

Many of my friends likewise seemed to reject me, or so I thought. More than my being rejected by them, I believe now that they were afraid of me, and in the end I probably rejected them too. Rejecting people was frequent and very easy for me to do. I cut no slack—one negative experience was all it took. Once I rejected someone, it was for good! I have gotten a lot better now, but I still struggle with that issue.

A few of my high school friends found ways to get out of going into the military. To this day I harbor bad feelings toward them. (Actually, I view them as chickenshit cowards.)

I had always wanted to be a teacher, but I couldn't afford college after high school. The military had been my ticket to an education, and I successfully pulled it off. Encountering teachers who'd gotten a college deferment to get out of the military and were not teaching due to their desire to teach triggered me beyond belief.

One quality I had to learn fast in the Nam was how to read people quickly. The desire to understand someone comes from the need either to understand them or to respect them enough to want to understand them. In Vietnam both cases

17

applied. Knowing and understanding my buddies, men in my squad, and to a degree my superiors were necessary. The quicker I gained this knowledge, the better my chances were for survival. I'm not sure I wanted to understand my civilian counterparts at all.

Communicating with me was also very difficult for a nonveteran. My vocabulary was different from his or hers. I was quick to anger—frequently for little or no apparent reason. Only other Vietnam veterans could understand my so-called reasons. I found idle conversation and a number of topics to be boring. When I was bored, I would either stare off in the distance or make some obscene comment. I also found a way to leave the area, either in my mind or in actuality. My age had remained the same, but Vietnam and combat had made my mind a century older.

The military had no provisions in place to normalize me back into society. I was fortunate that on my first tour the entire battalion was deployed. The majority of soldiers and marines were individually deployed, joined a unit, fought for a year or more, and were rotated home for reassignment or separation. When I arrived in San Francisco at Travis Air Force Base, still wearing my flak jacket and helmet, I was sent to Treasure Island and six days later released to become part of a world I had longed to return to. I had thought of little else during my two tours in country. I was expected to pick up where I had left off and appear unaffected by what I had seen, done, or experienced. Dream on!

All war is horrific, and each has its own dynamics. I would never try to compare one war to another; nor would I ever criticize a veteran of any war. Unless he has been there, no one can understand what forces impact a soldier in combat; nor can he imagine what he endured. Frequently, veterans who served side by side failed to understand why their buddy didn't perceive an event the same way they did.

For example, my first fire team leader and I remained the best of friends ever since serving together in Vietnam. He and I have talked often of both good and bad experiences that happened to us there. Even though we were literally side by side, many times our perceptions of an event varied greatly.

If I had trouble understanding how my buddy viewed a tangible event, how could I understand how that event had affected him? I couldn't! I just had to trust and be there for him just as we had been there for each other in Nam. I have come to realize that I can only speak of Vietnam, my experiences there, and the effects those experiences had on me. I wouldn't now, nor would I ever, try to impose my interpretation of an event on another Vietnam veteran. And if I wouldn't do this to another vet, why in the hell would I ever try to explain it to a civilian?

No one can expect a veteran to return from combat and be the same person he was before. That was expected of us, and for that matter we somewhat had that expectation of ourselves. No one told us any differently. We couldn't talk about Vietnam and in most cases didn't want to. Facing the consequences of acknowledging that we were Vietnam veterans also posed a social threat. So, we came home having spent days in the monsoons and having experienced red laterite dust, temperatures in the one hundreds, grueling assignments, the killing or wounding of friends, the lack of a front line, clothing rotting off, jungle rot, and many more unpleasurable experiences. The sad thing was that we could only internalize our emotions.

My days after my return home were considerably different but nonetheless agonizing. Home wasn't what I'd expected. When I left California, I dedicated myself to become a part of society. I didn't approach this goal in a halfhearted way. My ninth-grade history teacher, Nelly Smith, who looked remarkably like the painting of George Washington by Stuart, always quoted the phrase "The world is mine oyster with which sword I shall open." I felt like this phrase upon returning from Vietnam.

Then came the ambush! It wasn't the baggage I had brought home—all soldiers from any war bring home the demons of combat. To some degree I believe I expected those demons to remain with me for the rest of my life. What I didn't expect was the way I was received when I got home. I recognize that I may have had fantasy expectations. I'm not referring to those not being fulfilled. My ambush came from the real events that occurred in the pursuit of my oyster.

It probably would have come anyway, but I believe the ambush I came home to not only dashed some of my dreams but also set the stage for my demons to flourish.

CHAPTER THREE
The Firefight: My
Symptoms Surface

While the experiences and perceptions I internalized might differ greatly from those of other Vietnam veterans, they were mine. I brought them home like items in my seabag, and I had to try to live with them. This baggage included my guilt over what I had done to survive, survivor guilt, difficulty in grieving, depression for days at a time, hypervigilance, anger, lack of trust, and a need to guard and defend everything in my perimeter. The most devastating challenge for me was to trust others enough to give up control. I would come to recognize many years later that these were symptoms of PTSD. Many veterans suffered, and continue to suffer, other symptoms as well. Most, if not all, can be attributed to Vietnam and the aftereffects of our service there.

A PTSD symptom is an observable reaction to a traumatic event that took place earlier in one's life. My symptoms are a complex series of reactions I have to situations or events that, in some way, trigger my memories of incidents in Vietnam.

My symptoms are always dormant within me, and until I react to a trigger, they remain dormant. A symptom is like a big bass under a lily pad. It anxiously waits for a frog to jump in the water near its lily pad; then it strikes. The triggers that bring on the reaction are very predictable, and once released, they allow the whole PTSD cycle to run its course. To delay or stop the progression takes a form of intervention.

My symptoms manifest themselves in the following sequence. First, something triggers me to react—the frog jumping in the water. Each veteran reacts differently to different sets of triggers. They can be sensory based, action based, memory based, or emotion based. Regardless of the trigger, it elicits a reaction. My reactions usually take the form of an actual PTSD symptom.

At this point it starts to impact not only me but also anyone who happens to be around me. Many times my reactions are overt. However, my reaction can appear as an emotional event, such as withdrawing or sulking around. After demonstrating that I have lost control of myself, guilt can overwhelm me. In my case guilt always leads to depression. My depression may last for several weeks. Now the whole PTSD symptom has run its course, except for the days or weeks it takes me to recover from the depression.

PTSD symptoms are difficult topics to discuss. The difficulty becomes a twofold issue for me. Initially, I was concerned that the reader wouldn't understand the points I was trying to make. Second, I would have to bare my soul in describing them. These concerns were answered when I considered my audience. Veterans and people close to veterans would probably be my readers. These readers would understand what I was trying to say and how difficult it was to say it.

It has taken me a long time to analyze myself and recognize the character flaws I brought home from Vietnam, better known as my PTSD symptoms. I elect to call them "flaws," because the society I came home to didn't accept them. Looking back, I would have to agree that they were probably unacceptable in any society. Some of the behaviors, however, proved to be beneficial to me and to my effort to adapt. These included hypervigilance, skepticism when asked to trust, perimeter defense, and control. When I look at the positive aspects of my PTSD symptoms, I wonder if they weren't my way of accepting myself. For survival's sake, finding some value in my life was necessary. Since PTSD was part of my life, by accepting it, I was accepting myself. When I wasn't acknowledged for my military service and when the society I had come home to didn't accept me, I had to create that acceptance for myself. In the world of the civilians, hypervigilance equated to a heightened awareness to what was going on around me. Being skeptical when asked to trust was nothing more than being cautious of my dealings with others. Guarding my perimeter meant taking care of my family and possessions. Control, when I applied it to my responsibilities, wasn't a bad thing either.

Unfortunately, for me and most Vietnam veterans, moderation wasn't in our vocabulary. While these seemingly good traits were acceptable, I had the tendency to carry them beyond the acceptable level. If anyone questioned or contradicted my approach in handling a situation, they triggered any number of adverse reactions. If my perimeter was breached or I couldn't trust someone, my reactions always exceeded the norm. In most cases the bad outweighed the good. This was my mode of operation, and I believed in my approach. It didn't take much to trigger an overreaction on my part. The negative side of the symptoms I displayed far outweighed the positive side. In attempting to legitimize my PTSD symptoms, I had found a way to accept myself. The acceptance I found in myself allowed me to find value in my life—a life that didn't actually have much value.

Even as my symptoms were emerging rapidly, I tried to understand them. My analysis wasn't very successful, since it was generally done in the guilt-ridden stage of depression. A simple question haunted me: what came first—the chicken or the egg? Were my symptoms of control, hypervigilance, distrust, and anger all related to my wanting to guard my perimeters? Or were my control issues what forced me to set up perimeters and guard them with hypervigilance and reluctance to trust? Possibly I had become so hypervigilant in Nam that I felt secure only when I had established control of my perimeters. It would be easy to say that the symptoms and issues all act together. I'm convinced, at least in my case, that a primary symptom (control) governs the others. It took me a number of years to recognize that control was my primary symptom. I discovered it when trying to determine my number one stressor for the VA. All my symptoms pointed to one thing: control.

Control

I established perimeters in an effort to control all that took place within them. I used hypervigilant techniques learned in Nam to guard my perimeters. I was reluctant to trust, because trusting could allow an enemy within my perimeter. I controlled, or had some control over, my perimeters in Vietnam, and I attempted to maintain that same control over my stateside perimeters. Stateside, these perimeters were domains of my life and the lives of those around me. Everything became a domain I had to have some form of control over. Home, family, friends, activities, and my classroom were examples of domains I had to control. When looking at my life after Vietnam, I basically attempted to control all aspects of it. When I lost some element of control or found myself in a situation where I had no control over my destiny,

I became angry, became aggressive, turned to alcohol, or just ran from the area. I couldn't really battle the demons until I recognized my main issue was control.

I nearly always overreacted when something startled me or backed me into a corner. My three options were to fight, take flight, or submit. I found submitting to be almost impossible, and if I couldn't get away, either physically or mentally, the only option left was to fight.

The overreaction would unfold in the following way. I would become instantly on the defensive and in some manner, either vocally or physically, would try to fight my way out. Other situations that triggered an overreaction on my part included a violation of my trust, a threat to my perimeter, or an attempt to control me or my actions. Generally in these instances, I tried to distance myself from the person or persons who violated my rules (flight). I can assure you of one thing: submission was seldom, if ever, an option I chose.

Guilt

I always seemed to find a way to feel guilty for things I had done or for things I had left undone. Guilt is a heavy burden for me and, until the last several years, seemed to be just a part of my life. I actually looked for things to feel guilty about. If I couldn't find a reason to feel guilty, I would make one up. I believed in my heart that I was constantly hurting someone. Most people wouldn't view me this way, but deep within me I'm a very tender person who hates the thought of hurting anyone. During and after Vietnam, however, hurting others seemed like all I did. I was tired of hurting people, most of all those people I loved or cared about. To sum it up, I was tired of hurting myself due to my guilt feelings.

My contribution in taking the life of another human being was guilt that was difficult to resolve. In boot camp and in Infantry Training Rifles (ITR), what was instilled in me was that the enemy was of a subhuman culture. Therefore, I was to regard my enemies as subhuman. They were gooks, slants, dinks, and so forth. On the other hand, we weren't human to them. I recognize this philosophy is a necessary part of training for all war and takes place on either side. In World War II, for example, we fought the Krauts and Nips. The pathetic thing about this mind-set is that we must be brainwashed or traumatized to kill another human being. Killing is necessary for our own survival as well as that of the men we're serving with, but now the approach seems barbaric.

Anger also plays a huge role. Each soldier finds anger in the many sacrifices he has made and for the most part wants to take revenge out on the enemy. For civilians who have never been in that situation, there are many sacrifices they can't identify with, much less understand. The obvious sacrifices are easily recognized. The more abstract sacrifices, on the other hand, are generally insignificant to those who were not boots-on-the-ground soldiers. A few sacrifices would include the feeling of safety, a meal other than C rations boxed during the Second World War, and a dry place to sleep. For this sacrifice we were rewarded with wet feet, jungle rot, cuts that won't heal, red dust, and heat (to mention a few). To this day I hate lacing boots. Each time I pull a boot string, I'm reminded of how the laces only cut deeper into my fingers each time I laced my boots. The cuts on the insides of my fingers wouldn't heal. As a surveyor, reading the optics on my transit became detestable to me. If it wasn't the sweat burning my eyes, it was the struggle to keep rain off the lens. These are a sample of my abstract sacrifices.

Obvious sacrifices were common to all of us. They included missing our girls or wives, longing to see our families, missing the carefree lives we had known before the military and Vietnam, and generally not having to always be in harm's way. Each Vietnam veteran experienced his own hell, his own demons, his own fears, and his own feelings of sacrifice. These sacrifices are as individual as the soldier himself. Our sacrifices greatly contributed to a soldier being able to take the life of another human being.

When I saw a brother wounded or killed, I instantly hated the enemy and wanted him dead. We were all brothers, a name and a bond forged in respect, trust, and the value we placed on each other. To this day some forty-plus years later, I still consider all Vietnam veterans my brothers. The strength of that bond has been the single element that has allowed me to band with other Nam vets much like I did with my buddies in Vietnam. Brothers take care of each other. It is only to other vets that I can express my feelings of guilt and expect them to be understood. I gained these feelings in Vietnam and brought them home with me. Feelings that strong, that have lasted that long, explain the impact they had on me. Is it any wonder I wanted to take revenge on the enemy? Regardless, I had compromised the values learned in my youth. The conflict between the need to act as I did in combat versus the values I had grown up with created many of my guilt symptoms, while destroying a great amount of my self-worth.

Survivor Guilt

Survivor guilt is a specific type of guilt. What makes it different for me are the triggers that allow it to surface and the emotions I have when experiencing it. Unlike several of my symptoms, such as hypervigilance and control, my survivor guilt has diminished greatly in both frequency and intensity since Vietnam. There are three examples of survivor guilt I can relate to. By no means am I suggesting that there aren't others. Anyone's guilt feelings are based partially on his personal history and experiences in-country.

For most Vietnam veterans, the most devastating type of survivor guilt came when a buddy or

member of their unit was lost. They wondered,"
Why did I make it when my brother didn't?" There
are so many instances of this situation that one
could write a book on these examples alone. I
had a friend in another battalion who related his
survivor-guilt demon to me. He and two buddies
were exiting their hooch during a rocket attack.
He happened to be in the middle; the man in front
and the man behind him were severely wounded,
while he didn't get a scratch. Two other examples
deal with men who were detached to different lo-
cations; while they were gone, their replacements
were killed. These two men are friends of mine,
and their survivor guilt played a big part in their
PTSD. Finally, I felt guilty about feeling so high following a firefight, mortar attack, or rocket attack.
This euphoria didn't bother me at the time, but
later I would question my feelings." I have been
told this euphoric feeling was an adrenaline rush.
Rush or not, it made me feel guilty.

Grief

Grief is a very difficult topic and a struggle for
me to discuss. The inability to show grief affects
a high percentage of Vietnam veterans, including
me. My difficulty comes when I compare myself to
those grieving around me. I just don't understand
my feelings. When dealing with grief or knowing
how I should be dealing with it, I generally end
up feeling guilty. When I was young prior to my
military service, I was tenderhearted, and when

confronted with the death or injury of a loved one or anyone I knew, for that matter, I fought to hold back my tears. I remember this event so well because I didn't think men or boys were supposed to express their emotions that way. My World War II veteran father, who was with Patton's Third Army in the Battle of the Bulge, taught me this. I was embarrassed that I wore my emotions on my sleeve. Consequently, I felt grief and sadness but tried not to let my emotions show.

Anyone reading the last paragraph would clearly recognize that I don't believe a single event or a series of events alone can cause PTSD. My entire life contributed to each PTSD reaction when an event triggered me or a jeopardizing situation confronted me. No, PTSD didn't start with me in Vietnam. No one, including me, can exclude his or her personal history when looking at any element of PTSD. That's why there are so many different stressors with so many levels of severity. Each of us had a history prior to becoming a soldier. We had different spiritual beliefs, our value systems varied, we came from different cultures and subcultures, and our different life experiences greatly influenced how we evaluated a traumatic event.

After my two tours in Vietnam, I got to the point that I didn't have to try to suppress my grief. Not only had I evolved to the point of suppressing grief; I had, without knowing it, learned how to reject it. I hadn't lost my emotions and feelings, just my inability to show my grief to other human beings. It was like I'd brought home with me the "it don't mean nothing" syndrome. When my parents passed away, I felt guilty that I wasn't able to express my loss like others in the family. I loved my parents and felt terrible that they were gone. Believe me, I miss them with all my heart, and in some way I think about them daily, but to break down in tears at the funeral was impossible for me.

On the other hand, I would tear up very easily when pledging to the flag, hearing songs like "Amazing Grace," or singing the national anthem. These demonstrations of grief made me realize I still had the emotions of my youth. I just couldn't understand why it was so difficult for me to show those feelings when dealing with human loss. In turn, my lack of emotion made me feel so guilty. I can only reconcile this problem with the fact that I was trained not to show grief in the field. A soldier who takes time to grieve or even to think about grief is a liability to himself, his men, and the mission.

A firsthand example of my grieving process took place while I was writing this book. I mentioned earlier that my first fire team leader and I had remained very close friends since Vietnam. We were more than friends; we were as close as biological brothers. The dedication in this book details our brotherhood. I knew his death was coming, and I had a year and a half to prepare myself for it. I anticipated that his death would be a huge trigger and worried about how I would react.

Strangely enough, the situation wasn't any different from any other grieving event I had experienced since my service in Vietnam. He was on my mind ever since I heard of his passing and many months before, but I didn't express any open emotions. My entire family was concerned and sensed some hammer was about to fall. They didn't understand this part of me any more than they did my other PTSD quirks. Because I didn't talk about his death or show emotional grief, many family members and friends assumed I would go off the deep end. Surprisingly, to them I projected the image that his death was no big deal.

What they didn't realize was that my mind hadn't been off our relationship since I heard of his death. The things I thought about were private and personal between him and me. As I thought more and more about the times we had shared together, I decided to call several other members of our platoon and share with them that Gary had passed. The last time I had talked with either man was twenty years ago. We picked up where we had left off. It was as if time had stood still all those years. While we talked about our lives since Vietnam, our conversation included Gary. We didn't talk as though he was dead but rather shared a three-way phone conversation. There was absolutely no discussion about any bad experiences. When his name came up, it was in reference to some crazy thing he had done or some humorous situation he had gotten into. This conversation was what I wanted and needed. I'm certain that anyone other than Vietnam veterans would have expected something very different. When thinking about my behavior, I question the possibly that I didn't trust anyone else enough to share my feelings with him or her. In general I didn't want to talk to anyone about his death. My thoughts were private, and I was very careful whom I chose to share them with.

Hypervigilance

To the Vietnam veteran hypervigilance goes far beyond the range in the scope of most civilians. It is complex and varies both in intensity and in how it might manifest in the veteran. His duties in-country have had an instrumental impact on the level of hypervigilance he demonstrates upon returning home. The Vietnam veteran is hypervigilant not only about what goes on in his surroundings but also in his observation of people around him. My hypervigilance became so refined that only other Nam vets understood how refined it was. My senses were on full alert at all times.

These skills were introduced during boot camp and ITR. In boot camp paying attention to details and orders was emphasized. In ITR (military training) this skill was refined by honing my awareness of all that went on around me. Applying and refining these skills in Vietnam took little time for me. I found levels of sensory awareness I didn't even know existed. Most Vietnam veterans seem to possess this ability.

Last summer a Vietnam buddy was visiting my wife and me at our camp in Upstate New York. He observed that something was triggering me. He later told me about that observation. It was true! He had hit the nail on the head. My wife, children, and other friends around me didn't have a clue. He had sensed and observed cues others had totally overlooked. The awareness my buddy demonstrated was typical of a Vietnam veteran.

I suffer from extreme anxiety when I find myself in large groups. Crowds and where I place myself in these crowds greatly affect my anxiety level. The duties I had in Nam are reflected in how severely I react to that anxiety. Men who spent time in the bush or had a lot of convoy duty have a tendency to always ensure they have a means of exit. They will situate themselves close to doors, exit signs, and doorways. On the other hand, I spent the majority of my combat time defending a fire base, base camp, installation, or project. I wanted to ensure that my back was secured and that only friendlies were behind me. I won't be found in the middle of a room, in seats in the center of a restaurant, or in any place where I could be approached from behind. The severity of a veteran's hypervigilance is in direct correlation to the level and duration of hypervigilance he needed to feel secure in-country.

Hypervigilance is one of the symptoms I find most difficult to control. I seem to carry an extra amount of hypervigilance with me at all times. My senses make me more aware of what goes on around me and of potential things that could go wrong within my perimeter. I don't believe the average person possesses this ability or need, nor does he probably want to. In addition to constant hypervigilance, I'm subject to having my hypervigilance aroused by a number of triggers. Hypervigilance is controlled internally through processing all of my senses. This processing suppresses conscious choices of the fight, flight, or submit responses. It's mainly controlled internally, and once it became part of my makeup, it was impossible for me to manage or control. It's just there, and I use it whether I want to or not. Here's one example. When I find myself in a crowd, my eyes dart all over, people almost become a blur, and I sometimes sweat. I'm so anxious that I feel like exploding. I can't seem to be able to reduce these reactions, and as a result, they become a very difficult issue for my family. This symptom greatly affects me, and I consider my case to be on the very high hypervigilance scale.

Why am I this way? I believe I can answer this question by explaining my duties in Vietnam. I said earlier that I had been a surveyor in the Seabees. As an NCO, I was usually a crew leader. This meant that I was responsible not only for the job assignment but also for two to five men. Our surveying jobs would take us into villages, on roads, to bridge constructions, into Hue City, and into many other assignments and project sites. Surveying is a technical job requiring a great amount of attention to detail and accuracy. Now, couple that demand with ensuring safety for my crew. I couldn't let my guard down for an instant, or I would jeopardize the safety of my crew and the quality of the job we were doing. Before taking a crew out, I had to evaluate the job, prepare equipment, and brief the crew. Likewise, I had to select needed weapons (frequently, one or two of my crew carried shotguns while working in villages), C rations, and any auxiliary gear my crew might need. If I could round up an extra crew member, which was rare, I added him to the crew for security. The pressure I had as a survey crew leader forced me to be hypervigilant both before and throughout the time I had my crew on a job assignment. My military duties as a squad leader were no different than those of any other NCOs and officers who had to lead men in combat. One who has been there knows that hypervigilance is the bonding agent that gains respect from his men by helping to ensure their safety in combat.

Anger

Another problem (symptom) I have difficulty with is anger. Anger has probably gotten me into more immediate trouble than any other symptom. I actually experience two types of anger. The first is the spontaneous outburst. The second is the slow boil.

The spontaneous outburst usually results from my being backed into a corner or being confronted on the spot (blindsided). When I'm blindsided, the only option I have is to fight back. It doesn't matter how many tools I have learned to use to combat PTSD symptoms; I can't seem to be able to use them in this situation. My anger comes on so quickly that I react without thinking. As I mentioned previously, we have only the options of flight, fighting, or submission. Being backed into a corner or being blindsided doesn't offer flight as an option, and submission is almost out of the question. What is left? I fight back. The adrenaline rush of fighting back is similar to the adrenaline rush following combat. The sad part about fighting back is that even though at times I might have appeared to win, I've lost. If I'm lucky enough not to end up in jail, I do little more than show others I can't control myself. Control is so important to me, but in these situations, I can't control myself. I either instilled fear in those around me, or people lose respect for me. Fighting just classifies me as another crazy Vietnam veteran.

For me the slow boil is worse than spontaneous anger. A slow boil can be a coming event, a situation I sense might trigger me, or, worse yet, an accumulation of small triggers. When the triggers come in small increments, the intensity of my anger becomes more intense. If I'm in a conversation and find someone being offensive, each time he or she speaks, I become more agitated. At some point I explode.

The difference between the slow boil and spontaneous anger is that the slow boil gives time to choose one of the two options other than to fight. The slow boil isn't like being backed into a corner or being hit cold; I have the option to submit and not let the situation bother me, or I can remove myself from the situation. However, if I were to choose the fight option, an instantaneous strategy or plan would be formed. My spontaneous anger almost always brings on an overt reaction. The slow boil, on the other hand, tends to be more covert. My covert reactions take the form of revenge on the person or entity that triggered me. While the time prior to my reaction gives me the opportunity to think, it also gives me time to plan. Most plans are formulated in such a manner that they ensure in my mind that I will probably win or come out on top.

Several years ago my wife and I went to a local high school football game. Our youngest daughter played in the band, and we really wanted to see her march. During the entire season, both my wife and I had worked in the Band Boosters concession stand, which hadn't allowed us to watch her. For the last home game of the season, we got people to stand in for us during the game. We went early to help with the concession stand before the gates opened. Just prior to the gates opening, we selected two seats in the general admission area. From these seats we had a very good view of the field. But when the crowd came in, a group of several people sat directly in front of us. During the entire pregame the man in front of my wife stood. My wife couldn't see at all but didn't say anything. His behavior continued through the first half. During the halftime show, my wife asked him politely to sit down so she might be able to see. He responded, "No" and continued by saying that she had taken his seat. He said that he always sat there and that she had no right to take his seat. Mind you, this was general admission seating. My wife explained that nicely, but still he remained standing. At this point I became aware of the situation and got involved by nicely asking him to sit down. He didn't respond, so we stood behind him.

Now I evaluated the situation and developed my plan. My mind was blank except for my concentration on him and the group he had with him. Before I enlisted in the military, I had taught judo at the YMCA. I hold a black belt, and even though my training was many years ago, I haven't forgotten the techniques. I considered this man's age, his physical characteristics including his hands (smooth and soft), anyone with him who might be a threat, and their location. I now made eye contact with him constantly and from time to time nudged him. He appeared very uncomfortable but elected to say or do nothing. I was begging for him to make a move or say anything. My plan was to throat chop him and strike his brother with a palm blow to his nose. That would disable them both without a lot of effort on my part. As we left the game, I positioned myself behind and above him on the bleachers. On the way down, I bumped him repeatedly. Fortunately, nothing happened.

My wife knew I was upset but couldn't believe I was ready to react that way. Her alarm made me afraid to think about what I could have done. During the whole time I'd felt like a coiled spring. It wasn't a pleasant feeling, and I pray to God I don't allow it to happen again. The situation made me so aware of what could have happened that I believe now I might choose a different option. I can't say for sure. I shared this story with my PTSD group and concluded that I had to figure out tools to help me handle a situation of this type.

In some respects my anger is justified. As a Vietnam veteran, I have so many things to be angry about, and I realize the anger has to be channeled or redirected into something that becomes positive. The Vietnam Veterans of America did so when it adopted the slogan "Never Again Will One Generation of Veterans Abandon Another." This slogan gives the Vietnam veteran the opportunity to channel his anger into something positive: a cause and a purpose.

Before my anger could be rechanneled, I had to first figure out where it had come from. It took me decades to figure this out and then only with the help of my very good Vietnam buddies. Until I came to understand my anger and its origin, it was a demon hiding within me. I'm still plagued by never knowing when the demon will come out. After years of pent-up anger, I believe I have identified its source. I get angered by—and don't trust—most authority figures. I resent those in the country who didn't support us when we returned from Vietnam. I detest the establishment that refused us jobs and positions we had been promised. Most of all, I feel we were denied the acknowledgment, validation, and acceptance we deserved. These events were totally out of my control. How is it possible *not* to get angry over these issues? Anger isn't the problem. The way I sometimes handle it is!

Trust

Most people would define *trust* as the confidence or faith one has in a person or thing; to depend on. To the Vietnam veteran, in particular, trust is more than a definition that sounds good and can be bent around someone's self-serving wants or needs. In Vietnam trust was a sacred value. As much as you needed to be able to trust your buddies, you needed to know your buddies trusted you. Trust varied slightly, depending on your rate or rank. (Remember, this is coming from the perspective of an E-5 squad leader or survey crew leader.) I will attempt to describe both the similarities and differences at the same time. It is not uncommon to look at something only as it affects you and only through your own perspective. I've spent a lot of time with brothers holding other rates and ranks, and I hope to represent them accurately when I generalize.

Soldiers recognize the need for trust between themselves and their immediate buddies. The same type of trust is desired at the command-or-leadership level. However, trust becomes more removed and more complex or broad in scope as you move from fire team leader to unit command. The higher up the chain of command, the more leaders must trust in men who are not actually at their side. Like the fire team leader, higher levels of command are still responsible for their men; there are just more of them. In addition, in Vietnam leaders always had to trust that their men would accomplish the mission. A solid background in leadership training or exposure to good leadership examples and experiences made the difference between a successful and unsuccessful leader. Mutual trust is essential for unit survival and mission success. A leader in Vietnam needed to trust his men, and his men needed to trust him.

I can't discuss command trust without touching on leadership styles. I became aware of the leadership styles in the military, and several years later they were reinforced in a psychology classroom at OSU. I would venture to say that all men who have served in the military have experienced the five leadership types. The type-one leader leads only by authority and commands by flaunting his or her rate or rank. Type two leads by threats and negative consequences. His or her opposite, type three, leads by promising rewards to his men or women. The fourth and equally bad type of leadership is the superior who attempts to lead by becoming buddies with his or her subordinates.

I believe most veterans would agree that none of these forms of leadership worked well in combat or in any leadership role. The most effective form of leadership comes from the superior who demonstrates leadership by example. At times leaders at any level may find it necessary to use any and all of the five leadership styles, since some situations dictate different approaches. However, a leader whose primary leadership style is leading by example gains optimum respect and trust from the men or women he or she leads. I learned this truth early in life and attempted to apply it to my leadership roles in the military. My examples may seem simple, but I felt they helped me earn respect from my men. My men knew I would never ask them to do anything I wouldn't do myself. When I drew C rations for the squad, for example, I always took the last one. My men never stuck me with ham and beans; they knew I hated them. This may sound silly, but little things like that make a difference in leadership and trust in a leader.

The Perimeter

When leaving high school and prior to entering the military, I viewed perimeter as a math term meaning the distance around something. During boot camp and other advanced military training, I became familiar with a slightly different definition of the word. The new application had a much greater meaning. The something within the pe-rimeter now referred to men and security. Once I arrived in Vietnam, how important my perimeter actually was quickly became obvious.

In Vietnam the distance around me meant I was in an area I somewhat controlled. It was secure in that I knew what that perimeter contained. The strength and number of personnel were known. I knew the armament at my disposal and how it could best be used. I was aware of the terrain and the best way to defend it. As important as terrain was, the fact was that I generally had time to alter it to my defensive advantage.

Some units weren't given the opportunity to form elaborate perimeters. Besides the terrain, the quality of the perimeter depended on how much time I had to prepare it. When encounter-ing the enemy, patrols or units on the move had to make do with what was available. Frequently, man power was nearly all we had to work with in situations like these. It is difficult for me to totally appreciate or understand how my brothers who faced this situation on a daily basis dealt with it. On rare occasions, while on surveying projects, we had to form quick perimeters. This event was seldom and usually resulted from heavier-than-normal sniper fire or the premonition of impend-ing action.

On the other hand, I was on base camp perim-eters for most of my two tours. This duty differed a great deal from that of finding a quick perimeter, which I experienced only on jobsites and some surveying assignments. Seabees had the advantage of possessing heavy equipment to aid in building great perimeter defenses. Zigzag trenches not only provided some safety from grenades and mortars but also made positioning interlocking fire much easier. There were several disadvantages, however. One was that it was difficult for a squad leader to see what was going on with two of his three fire teams. Listening posts were very different from those in the field. A trench went straight to within a few feet of the wire, perpendicular from a zigzag. We sent only one man on listening post at a time. The squad leader was in charge of who was selected and how long he would remain in that position. To me assigning a man to listening-post duty was the most dreaded assignment I had to make. I'm not exceedingly brave, nor am I a great leader, but I refused to ask a man to do anything I wouldn't do myself. During the first night as a squad leader in a combat situation, I took the position of listening post. My first fire team leader had the squad. After that night, putting a man in that situation always bothered me.

The Tet Offensive in 1968 gave a whole new meaning to perimeter defense. It was like going from Little League baseball directly to the big leagues. The Gia Le combat base had no exit route, so our perimeter had to be defended at all cost. Sometimes the cost was great.

Perimeters were such an important part of my survival, and their value was so emphasized, that

I could never leave them in Vietnam. Once I was home, my perimeters became different but were no less important than they had been in Nam. I felt like my perimeters were necessary for me to function. They had evolved from an area around my combat base to anything I thought I had to protect. Only then did I have the sense of security and safety.

I could probably write a book on what Vietnam veterans view as their perimeter and what they feel belongs within that perimeter. They range from small items like a shoebox to something as large as a farm or lake. They may be items or space and even people. Many Veterans view values, ideas, and methods of doing something as items in their perimeter. As in Vietnam, a veteran will defend and protect everything in his perimeter. Perimeters are more critical to him, so it's likely that his defense of them will be stronger than that of the average civilian.

When the VA determined that I had to complete a stressor letter, I went to my Veterans Service Office for guidance. My veterans service officer instructed me on the process and gave me the application to take home and complete. The application looked simple until I started to fill it out. Basically, all I had to do was identify my primary and secondary stressor. I take things like forms and applications very literally, a fact leading to my next big dilemma.

"What happened in Vietnam that brought on your problems?" This seems like a simple question, but as I thought about the many contributing events that could have been a cause, I found each to be lame. In my mind no one event seemed traumatic enough in itself to cause my problems. More importantly, I didn't want to think about those events, much less share them. Individually, they seemed trivial compared to action or events many of my brothers had gone through. Some of my buddies were in combat nearly every day they were in-country. My combat time was only about forty days in two tours. I was embarrassed to describe my combat experience, since it didn't compare to theirs. What I hadn't put into the equation were the sniper rounds fired as harassment while I was on surveying jobs as well as the constant vigilance necessary to counter the threat of booby traps and mines. These threats were real, and whether I counted them as combat or not, I was affected all the same. Sharing these experiences was also embarrassing, because I felt they showed a sign of weakness. That too came from Vietnam. I never felt like I could show weakness or fear while in-country, and I hesitate to show it now. I would much rather consider myself as one who was unaffected by combat and just did what had to be done.

Unlike many Vietnam veterans who could identify a single event or one repeated event, I was unable to narrow down to a single stressor. I looked at each symptom from a published list in several books. I felt like I was being asked to misrepresent myself. I could relate to almost all situations and events expressed in the books. They had happened either to me or to someone around me during my tours. Identifying any one event would require me to lie, exaggerate, or embellish the effect it had had on me. While struggling to find that single stressor, I had to examine my feelings and analyze all of them and how each had impacted me at the time. As I went through them one by one, I began to realize there was one common thread in all the symptoms that kept surfacing. That element was control. Whether it was grief, guilt, survivor guilt, hypervigilance, trust, or guarding my perimeter, control was the core issue that kept surfacing.

The type of control I'm referring to is not the typical interpretation. It has nothing to do with the necessity to be in charge. To me it has to do with my being able to control my environment. At last I had determined my stressor.

I turned the page, and the next question confronted me. "What is your second stressor?" Since I was mentally exhausted from determining stressor one, I thought, "How in the hell can I go through this again?" I quickly selected my plane ride home from Vietnam and halfheartedly filled in the lines. The thought of this senseless exercise triggered me into a depression that lasted for several days.

CHAPTER FOUR
Corpsman, I'm Hit!:
Intervention

My choices of interventions started the day I was separated from active duty and continues to this day. Unfortunately, I wasted thirty-five years on meaningless or damaging types of intervention. Intervention is a two-headed coin. It's a word that had several meanings for me, depending on how far I had progressed in my recovery from PTSD. Before I realized PTSD ruled my life, a quick fix rather than an intervention would have been a more applicable way to describe what I wanted. There was one thing for sure: if I wasn't aware of the cause, I couldn't select an appropriate intervention. I was ignorant of PTSD and made many terrible choices where intervention was concerned. The majority of people think of intervention as a positive thing. They couldn't be more wrong.

For me intervention has always been needed to fight depression. For the last ten years, I have been aware that I suffer from PTSD. Once I became aware of it, selecting more appropriate and beneficial interventions became easier. The progress I've made in this area gives me hope that I'm slowly regaining what I consider to be a normal life—a real normal life, not one conjured up in a young Vietnam veteran's mind. The selection process for picking positive interventions also became more focused as now I realized what the main demon was. I had to eliminate or better manage my control issues and depression episodes. My depression is nearly always preceded by an event that triggers me to react. Most of my reactions aren't acceptable by society's norm, a fact that leads to my feeling bad or guilty for reacting as I do. Guilt always puts me into depression. Actually all PTSD symptoms put me into a depressed state. This is why getting a handle on it became so imperative. I will never stop seeking help or positive intervention to fight the depression demon.

Depression has been such a huge part of my life since Vietnam that you would think I would know how to deal with it by now. What makes it difficult is that depression is rarely a symptom by itself. Depression is the result of triggers impacting my life. The type of triggers and my reactions to them determine whether I go into a mild or severe depression. The severity of depression also dictates how long I will remain in it. I realize that while I'm in a depressed state, other variables can relieve or deepen the effect depression has on me.

"Withdrawal and isolation" seems to be the most common action I take when dealing with a depression. As well as just wanting to be alone, I wonder if I don't withdraw or isolate just to insulate myself from being subjected to additional triggers. While isolation may insulate me from external triggers, it by no means insulates me from triggers conjured up in my mind. Nearly everyone is familiar with various forms of depression. But as it affects me, I'm going to keep it in the scope of a Vietnam veteran. In regard to my PTSD, the reasons for my depression are very predictable. I should clarify myself by pointing out that predictability came to me only after I realized I had PTSD.

Depression is the tail end of my PTSD cycle. It takes a trigger to bring on a reaction from me. The reaction is to fight, flee, or submit. When I fight, my terminal goal is to win. Society once considered me a loser. I don't welcome that outcome again. Fleeing takes on many faces. I can literally run away to a garage, workshop, woods, or lake—or even within my own mind (the one-thousand-yard stare). In some way I must remove myself from the situation. Submission is seldom chosen as an option. Consequently, I tend to overreact or become literally numb when a response option confronts me. If I'm given a chance to think, my body becomes like a coiled spring, or I feel like I've got electric current running throughout my body. My responses are predictable and usually result in overreacting or going beyond what is acceptable by most standards. Once I regain control of myself, I realize I've gone too far and feel guilty for my actions. Guilt for my actions is an instant conduit to depression.

Depression can be the result of my feeling helpless in a given situation. News events I have no control over can also trigger depression. For me the most common problem is my guilt for overreacting. As I get older, I'm unable to do things I did in my youth. The thought that I'm not capable, wanted, or needed (if only in my mind) brings on depression. In Vietnam I was capable. I felt that my squad and crew wanted and needed me. I really don't feel that way now unless I'm with my Vietnam buddies.

Depression is such a dominating emotion that when I am in a depressed state, I don't think I can dig my way out. Given enough time, I can get out of most depressions on my own. Even though I can get out of them on my own, doing so takes me ten days or more. That is a long time to put me and my family through hell. When I feel like there is no way out, I will seek some form of intervention.

Depending on the severity and type of trigger, I sometimes need intervention immediately. Symptoms that commanded immediate intervention were spontaneous anger, invasion of my perimeter, and overload of my hypervigilance capabilities. When guilt, survivor guilt, grief, and trust are the symptoms, intervention is equally critical—but for a very different reason. These symptoms will develop more slowly and allow the coupling of other triggers to be added to what had initially triggered me. Trying to identify what had initially set me off made it that much more difficult to deal with. It's hard for me to sort out triggers when I'm faced with several at the same time. This is when intervention is greatly needed to help me sort them out. Most of the time I cannot recognize the initial trigger that set me off. My reactions to accumulated triggers are much more emotional. I can sulk, feel sorry for myself, and not be pleasant to be around. It isn't until I can identify the initial trigger that I'm able to start coming back from the depression.

Symptoms that involve trust issues give me time to actually plot what my reaction will be. Very often the reaction I choose will be one of finding revenge or getting even in some way. For Vietnam veterans this is a very dangerous position to be in. Intervention is needed as early as possible to help defuse the potential threat. I find that when I'm feeling the first signs, the ideal intervention is contacting a Vietnam buddy who understands the situation.

When I track my life with PTSD from 1968 to the present, I see that my choices of intervention become quite clear. If I were to put them on a scale ranging from zero (bad choices) to ten (good choices), it becomes obvious that my choices have evolved upward through the years. The evolution has developed as I've become more and more aware that I—not others—am the one with the problem. My choices became even better once I realized I had PTSD and became much better yet when I bonded with other Vietnam veterans, who like me suffered from PTSD. I could identify with these vets, and they could identify with me. We shared the same issues and problems. Moreover, there was an unspoken knowledge that understanding and help were best coming from someone who had walked in the same boots.

Veterans who choose interventions on the low end of the scale are making choices that aren't necessarily helpful and can be harmful to them and those around them. I believe these veterans are actually on a self-destructive path, with suicide being the extreme intervention choice. I'm familiar with suicide as a choice, since I can share two stories that are very close to me. A member of my squad committed suicide upon arriving home from his second tour in Vietnam. His experiences in Nam as well as his wife's filing for divorce several weeks after his return were the events that put him over the edge. Another friend worked with me at Western Electric and was in-country about the same time I was. His wife had left him while he was gone. She had taken everything as well as his military benefits until he was about to come home. He took what cash he had accumulated in Nam and purchased a new, very hot car. On the Friday night after getting his car, he drove down Broad Street at a very high rate of speed. He crashed into a concrete barrier.

No other vehicles were involved. Alcohol was said to be the cause. I will never believe that to my dying day. It is my belief that some veterans choose suicide as the intervention to rid themselves of the demons permanently.

I have never considered suicide in this manner. However, on many occasions I have thought about just walking away. I felt this would allow me not only to escape the demons but also spare my family from having to put up with me. The only thing that stopped me was the fear of hurting loved ones even more. I couldn't bear the thought of putting them through more pain than I had already subjected them to. I also felt this would be a form of submitting to the demons, and fighting them was much more my style. Who am I kidding? Walking away is a technique I practice on both a large and small scale. I escape to my hunting cabin almost four months a year. The thought of being alone was inviting when I was suffering depression or felt overrun by triggers.

On a smaller scale, there are times when I just escape to the woods or a lake. For me this is good. Some vets I talk to feel just the opposite. Alone time for them is negative and unleashes more demons. I have made tremendous progress recovering from my PTSD symptoms, but I still need the alone time and the solitude it offers. Thank God, my wife understands. She realizes the solitude offers me time to fight my demons without involving anyone else. She accompanies me to New York during the summer but is very tolerant about giving me the private time I need so desperately.

I only contemplated suicide by walking into the woods and never coming out. I can't say the same about alcohol and drugs. Once I realized alcohol temporarily buffered my pain, I quickly became addicted. Alcohol remained my intervention of choice for the next seventeen years. Any and all forms of alcohol could suppress my triggers, regardless of how small they seemed at the time. My problem with alcohol was that the effect would wear off, and I then had to consume more for the same high. In retrospect I can't recall any occasion when alcohol actually helped. I'm fortunate that I didn't kill myself or others during my years of drinking.

Some drinkers are said to be happy drunks. The only time I was a happy drunk was at the peak of my drinking escapade. I was triggered or depressed before I began to drink. That generally was why I started a drinking binge to begin with. When I was coming down from a drinking high, I was angry and more depressed than I had been before I started drinking. If during my drinking I made a real ass of myself, guilt made the depression even worse. Many of my actions while drinking could have easily landed me in jail or prison. Many Vietnam veterans have ended up incarcerated as the result of their intervention choices. If not for the grace of God, I could have easily joined their ranks.

During the end of my alcohol addiction, I became aware that drugs would produce the same effect, and I felt I could control them much more easily. I was only kidding myself. The people closest to me realized what I was doing. I never bought from the street but rather chose over-the-counter drugs. My methods of acquiring them were very efficient and in many cases devious. Alcohol and drugs, in my opinion, accomplish the same result as suicide. They just usually take longer to get the same results. These two addictions provide the veteran with more time to suffer and more time to inflict additional pain on those who love and care about him.

When I realized the demons I faced were mine, I started to make intervention choices that fell higher on my imaginary intervention scale. Even at this point, I chose interventions that were under my control. I had guarded my perimeter for so many years that I wasn't going to go outside of it now. I hadn't been able to shake that combat mind-set. It wasn't as clear to me then as it is now, but Vietnam was over. The only war for me to fight was the one within myself. I realized this, but I couldn't break the pattern. Control had become my security blanket.

One of the interventions I tried to use was self-discipline. It worked very well until a heavy trigger hit me. At that point I was right back where I had started. After fooling myself a number of times, I determined that something else was needed. I realized I still had big problems, but I couldn't figure out the cause or understand how to rid myself of the demons.

Manipulation is an intervention in itself, and believe me, I learned how to play that game well. It was common to manipulate my family and friends to believe they were to blame for my actions. I also manipulated many medical professionals to prescribe drugs that weren't actually needed. Manipulation is a necessary skill for a self-indulgent or selfish person. I feel ashamed to admit it, but at that point of my recovery, I was one of those people.

It's embarrassing but true that I have been selfish throughout my struggle with PTSD. I can look back now and recognize just how selfish I actually was and in some respects still am. Initially, I would blame my lot in life on everything and everyone else. I sought acceptance and acknowledgment but failed to accept and acknowledge others. I expected people to conform to my beliefs and ways of approaching things but wouldn't accept their ideas or methods. I wanted people to understand me but refused to appreciate their need for being understood. I feel as though I've recovered a great deal from PTSD. In fact, I view myself as being in maintenance mode. The selfish side of me now expects those around me to recognize I have PTSD and, based on that, to cut me some slack.

I vividly recall the next stage of PTSD in my life. I should, since it lasted ten years. I recognized there was something wrong, but I didn't know what it was. I thought I could fix the problem myself and was somewhat torn between blaming myself and blaming others. My choice was to blame others

for triggering me. After all, isn't it always easier
to blame others? In my heart I knew the demons
were within me, but blaming others removed my
responsibility for my actions and feelings. That
method didn't work well, since those around me
knew the problem wasn't their fault. At times I may
have been successful pulling this blame game off,
but for the most part, I fooled no one. The old saying tells it best: "You can fool some of the people
all the time and all of the people some of the time,
but you can't fool all the people all the time." I
found this statement to be so true in my case. On
the other hand, I was successful at manipulating
and fooling many doctors into giving me codeine
(Tylenol 3) for migraines, knee pain, tooth pain,
and damned near any pain I could conjure up. I
would use codeine to reduce my anxieties brought
on from PTSD symptoms. We took family trips to
Canada each summer. I would buy Tylenol with
codeine since it was sold over the counter in that
country. Consequently, I would purchase bottles
there to bring home for the same purpose as
prescribed codeine. The Canadian codeine was a
weaker dosage, so it took about one thousand pills
to last a year. I justified my actions because codeine
worked. I felt good without alcohol, which satisfied
my wife and family. What I didn't realize was that
I was only putting a Band-Aid on a much bigger
wound.

The closer I got to the realization that I
had PTSD, the more beneficial my choices of

interventions became. Going back to my scale, I see that at eight through ten I started seeking real help and real solutions. My most needed and beneficial intervention was forming relationships with other PTSD veterans. By bonding with my brothers, I realized I wasn't alone. As if I were in-country, it allowed me to join a squad, a new squad with two objectives. These objectives were, first, helping the individual veteran's recovery and, second, helping other veterans also recover from PTSD. I have no intention of putting down other professionals, individuals, or groups who try to help veterans. Many gains can be made from their dedication and efforts. However, when faced with our demons, we tend to turn to each other first.

Now I was ready to start reaching out to entities other than my brothers. This usually happened as the result of a recommendation from one of our brothers. These entities included my Veterans Service Office (VSO), the Veterans Administration (VA), and various veteran organizations. The VSO and VA provide professional help, while veteran organizations and counseling groups provided me with support and insight from veterans like me.

Reaching this level of recovery reassured me that I was actually becoming somewhat normal again, a feeling I had almost forgotten. PTSD is part of me and will always be there. Fortunately, the interventions I have chosen at this stage have enabled me to acquire more weapons to help and not hinder my battle with the demons.

CHAPTER FIVE
A Friend in the Foxhole:
The Value of a Buddy

Marines and Seabees call the foxhole a fighting hole. For the sake of poetic justice, I titled this chapter "A Friend in the Foxhole." It took me many years to evolve to the point that I could write the previous paragraphs. I have to thank a few of my Vietnam veteran buddies for helping me to see where I was and walking with me on the trail home. Without their help and patience, I would still be in the abyss that had been part of my life for more than three decades. I feel this is the appropriate place to express my gratitude. In the intervention section, I introduced the need for buddies on my journey home. I stressed that making meaningful progress wouldn't have been possible without their help.

In this chapter I have two purposes. First, I mean to describe how I perceived friendship before Vietnam and the agonizing years that followed my service there. Second, I want to pay tribute and express my gratitude to the men whose caring, giving, honesty, and guidance contributed greatly to the writing of this book. Without their help I would never have seen the corner, much less turn around it. Once I turned the corner, I realized that a number of others had contributed greatly to my recovery and a more fulfilling life.

While growing up, I had two best friends, and we remain best friends to this day. While we seldom see each other, we would be there if any of the three needed help. Our families didn't have much wealth in the form of money, but they were rich in values. We were World War II babies, raised to recognize that we had a duty to God, our country, and humanity. Hard work and honesty were the tickets to our future. All three of us served in the military, which enabled us to gain an education through the GI Bill. One of these friends is a retired attorney and judge. The other is a retired telecommunications engineer, the same construction electrician in MCB 53, which transported John and me to the 15th Aeroport in Da Nang, when we found ourselves stranded there.

Describing my relationship with other friends prior to my military service isn't difficult. I had many friends. While they weren't like my best friends, who were a constant in my life, my many other friends accumulated based on my varied interests. I was drawn to a particular group based on my interest at a given time. As my interest changed,

I was drawn to another group of friends. I always maintained the friends from the previous interest, so my friends accumulated throughout my adolescence. Consequently, when I entered the service, I had a number of friends. There were friends from places where I worked, friends from activities I enjoyed, and groups I enjoyed associating with. I would guess that most people considered me fun to be around, willing to try most things, creative involving activities, and very accepting of others.

It took very little time after arriving in Vietnam to realize that friendship there had an entirely different definition. Gone were the days when I could be close to a friend one day and move on to other friends the next. It wasn't like a sandlot basketball game with one set of friends and a weekend party with another set. While those friends were important to me, they didn't have the value I placed on my buddies in Vietnam. A guy could leave the basketball court, and his leaving had a minimal impact. That choice wasn't an option in-country. The level of commitment to buddies and the value placed on each other's life, I believe, were the primary differences. My buddies were some things within my perimeter.

I recall how I felt about someone new coming into that perimeter. Rate and rank made no difference. I felt the same about a new company commander as I did about a new squad member. While I tried to execute my duty, I resented the fact that I had to adjust to a new person. I don't fully understand why I felt this way, but I did nevertheless. I suspect this resentment came from the fact that new guys (FNGs) didn't make me comfortable. To gain comfort with a new guy meant he had to gain experience quickly or had to be trained. The jobsite and the perimeter wasn't a place where you wanted to train a new guy. The hypervigilance needed to survive would be sacrificed in the process. The bottom line was that you didn't want to jeopardize your security and the security of other men in your charge.

Comparing my best buddies in Nam to my lifelong friends at home is difficult. The friendships were forged under very different circumstances. When I try to discuss my three best Vietnam friends, my grief over their deaths begins to surface. All three died of cancer: two were confirmed with cancer resulting from exposure to Agent Orange, and the third had cancer from jet fuel (JP4) burns. I bonded with the three in very different ways.

Clarkie should never have been in Vietnam. He hated the military for taking him from his wife and his life back home. We spent a lot of time together in Country and Western bars. He would get drunk and play his guitar and sing. He had played in a band before the military and was very good. He would do anything for me, and I felt he needed a friend to look after him. He wasn't in my squad in Nam, but I tried to look after him as much as I could. He tied up with a dental tech, who was able to get him all the drugs he wanted. These habits came home with him, and between drugs and alcohol, his life was ruined. When he died in 1989, he left me his .270 deer rifle.

Chuck "Hiney-hole" was my philosopher buddy. In Chu Lai ('66–'67), we had racks together in the same hooch at base camp. When idle time presented itself, Hiney passed the time by sharing his numerous philosophies of life. His favorite topics included women, marriage, and the values of being a nudist. He danced to a different drummer, and his legacy was the many memories of topics we discussed and the crumpled eight point cover he wore while running a transit. He died in 2006 from a rare form of leukemia attributed to exposure to Agent Orange

Gary "Grim" was my best friend, as you would conclude from the dedication of this book. If two men could have been closer friends, I couldn't imagine it. Two tours together in Nam were followed by a lifelong friendship. We both suffered from PTSD, but Grim never recognized it in himself. I repeatedly tried to help him, but he was so resistant that a slight wedge formed between us toward the end of his life. I don't believe he could understand how I had changed. I'm sure this fact hurt him as much as it did me. I had acknowledged PTSD and wanted more out of life. I had lost too many years to the demons, and I wanted this peace for my friend also. Grim died of leukemia in 2012 from burns sustained while retrieving a transit and gear after a JP4 fuel bladder ruptured on Colco Road east of Hue City in 1968.

My wonderful wife, Patty, deserves more credit than I could ever put into words. I'm not sure whether I married a saint or an angel. We met and were married at the peak of my PTSD problems. Initially, I hid them well, but early in our marriage, they began to surface. She was committed to me and never gave up on the possibility that I would get better. Thanks to her, I came to realize that my life was much better than I thought. I had people who loved me and wanted nothing more than for me to recognize their love and be happy with my life. My wife is the kind of woman who would have been beside me in the fighting hole if she could have. She has certainly been by my side since our marriage in 1988. She endured my fits of anger, alcoholic years, nightmares, control issues, and the many other quirks brought on by PTSD. My wife has, and is, much more than a spouse and mother; she is my very best friend.

The real foxhole friends are my Vietnam buddies who have been at my side throughout my firefight with the demons. For the remainder of the book, I refer to my Vietnam buddies frequently. Without them I would still be lost in my world overshadowed by PTSD. The initial Vietnam Veterans of America (VVA) meeting I attended changed my life. It put me into contact with men like me—men I could relate to, men who understood me. They were by my side during my struggles with the Veterans Administration (VA) and the Department of Defense (DOD). When I became triggered, they helped defuse my anxiety. I was included in a group of veterans dedicated to fighting PTSD. As we progressed, our group evolved into a social network that included our wives. To this day we are no different from any other group of friends. We just all happen to be Vietnam veterans.

When I look at other groups, I see people who tend to enjoy each other's company. They may work together, be neighborhood friends, or be a gathering of family members. The point is that they aren't any different than we are. While we will always have PTSD, it no longer controls our lives. We need to stop labeling ourselves as PTSD veterans and recognize that we're just a group of people who enjoy being together. Granted, we share things other groups will never know or understand. The most striking difference is that we will always be there for each other. The bond we formed by serving in Vietnam is lasting, and that brotherhood will exist to our dying day.

In my ongoing quest to rid myself of the demons, two additional entities must be recognized. They are not particular individuals; nor are they totally made up of Vietnam veterans. First, my Veterans Service Office was an instrumental force in filing VA claims and helping me fight the DOD in getting the medals I deserved. Over the years personnel have changed, but not once was I rejected when asking for help. The second is my Friday morning PTSD group at our local VA clinic. The social worker who leads the group is one of the kindest, most caring persons I have ever met. She is perfect for those of us she works with. Thanks to her, I was able to rid myself of one of my stressors. The two-hour group, which she leads each Friday morning, possesses an atmosphere of trust and comradeship all who attend look forward to.

CHAPTER SIX
Operation Normal II:
My Continued Quest for Normal

I'll pick up my personal story with the birth of my first daughter in 1969. Once again, I thought all was going well. Following my workshop at Ohio State University and prior to my teaching position starting in the fall, we purchased an old farm west of Newark, Ohio. We had to build three rooms onto it before receiving a certificate of occupancy. I was able to handle that challenge as well as to continue my OSU classes and start a new teaching position. In my mind I felt wonderful about myself and thought others would accept me and be proud of me for my accomplishments. We had little money, but with my work ethic, I wasn't worried.

For the next seven years, I continued to think all was going well. We had two more children. My wife was a stay-at-home mother with the three kids. I had continued in college and received a bachelor's degree in vocational education (cum laude).

My teaching was going extremely well, and I had gradually made a great number of improvements to the old farm. However, money was always an issue during those seven years. I was too proud and reluctant to give up control and allow either my wife or others to help. I didn't recognize at the time that I had actually rejected their offers to help me. For reasons I didn't understand at the time, I would have rather just done it all myself. The challenge didn't bother me, because I regarded it as my duty. Believe me, if I had a duty, I followed it through to completion. Like any action or set of actions, there are always two sides. I was blind to the problems developing in the family unit. I was so convinced that I was making the right decisions that I couldn't imagine there was a negative side to what I was doing or that there could be any other way of doing it. In my effort to make my life normal, as I perceived normal to be, I was oblivious to all other options or suggestions. I was so self-focused in my quest that I took time only to adjust my blinders.

During the school year I would take between twelve and twenty credit hours of course work per quarter. Taking this load was necessary, since I was on the GI Bill and had to carry a full load to get reimbursement from the government. I taught my regular high school classes as well as two apprenticeship classes in the evenings. During some semesters I taught a four-hour apprenticeship class on Saturday. During the summers and on breaks, I would contract to build garages, build decks, and bid on insurance repair jobs. For two summers I worked for Kaiser Aluminum as a production relief foreman. On top of that, we raised a one-acre garden. We had an egg business and always had around one hundred chickens. Eggs were sold year-round, and when the hens quit laying, they were butchered and sold as stewing hens. At the end of my seventh year of teaching, I was given the opportunity to work as a consultant for a man who owned four companies—a lumber yard, a construction company, a roof-truss plant, and a prefabricated-home plant. I consulted for all four. The money was great and enabled us to purchase one of the homes I had been general contractor for. Most weeks consisted of working one hundred hours.

The time I had left to spend with my children was quality time, and I thank God for that. When I was at home or wasn't consumed by work, I did fun activities with the kids. A balance of work and play was always stressed, and both their mother and I likewise emphasized a strong value system. The children had a number of chores around the farm, but I did try to make sure fun and rewards were part of the work. For enjoyment I took them to stock auctions, built dams on the creek, went fishing, and did other activities that involved the kids. I always made an effort to introduce the kids to fun, learning, and work—in that order. I always tried to plan activities the children and I could share. With all my mistakes, I believe I did a fairly good job as a father. All six children have a wonderful work ethic. Four have families that would make any parent proud. Their chosen professions required college degrees, with four having advanced degrees. They have terrific value systems and show respect to people. I'm so thankful to God for this blessing.

If you look at the last several paragraphs, you'll note that I didn't mention my wife. She was safely in my perimeter, but I took for granted that she was OK with the way things were going. It didn't occur to me how inconsiderate I was of her and how I neglected her needs. The assumption I made would cost me my marriage seven years later. I left her to tackle her many responsibilities and honestly put all my other mixed-up priorities before her. In my stupidity I thought she should be proud of our progress. In actuality what she wanted was a husband who would give her time and attention. She is a wonderful person and a great mother, and she was a good wife. If she had a fault, it was that she didn't communicate her feelings to me. Possibly, I wouldn't have listened, or she may have been afraid to discuss the problem with me.

We were in a new home, the kids were getting older, and it seemed as though I had more time with the family. But I didn't realize that the feelings my wife once had for me were gone. While I'm a very hypervigilant person, I wasn't very vigilant concerning my wife's perspective of our marriage. With what I thought was idle time was time I should have spent trying to fix a damaged marriage. Instead I started taking graduate classes and putting a teaching résumé together. This pursuit lasted for another four years before my world caved in on me.

At this point we had been married eleven years and had two daughters and a son at ages ten, eight, and six respectively. I came home from work one day, and my wife said, "I don't love you, and I want a divorce." Her words totally hit me cold. I was devastated and begged her for a chance to rectify anything I had done wrong to save our marriage. I mentioned earlier that she was a poor communicator; thus, she had stored up everything until that moment when she announced her feelings toward me. I should have known a divorce was imminent but elected to leave it in her hands and go on trying to fix things as long as I could. I had hopes that like everything else, I could fix my marriage. In her mind she wanted me to pursue the divorce. With these two philosophies in place, we stayed together for another three-plus years.

During that time there was no resemblance of a marriage. If she'd wanted to get back at me during that time, she certainly did. We lived separate lives in the same house. She talked to me only by orders and negative comments. Other than working and playing with the kids, I led a solitary life. In addition there was no intimacy at all in my life. At one point my father suggested that I find someone on the side. My response to Dad was that if I was trying to fix the marriage, cheating on my wife would only make things worse. The next devastating part of the story is so humiliating that I'm embarrassed to tell it. In addition to being humiliating, it devoured the next seventeen years of my life and affected the lives of loved ones and friends.

During the latter part of this three-year period, I caught the flu. In an effort to get some rest, I purchased a bottle of NyQuil and that night took a healthy dose. I had suffered from insomnia ever since I returned from Vietnam. That night I got the best night's sleep I'd had in years. Sleep was so great that I stretched my new remedy through several more bottles. Then I realized it was the alcohol in NyQuil that had sedated me. I purchased a bottle of vodka and used it at night after the kids went to bed. This began my use of alcohol for all the wrong reasons. Up to that time, I had drunk socially but never because I felt I needed to. Alcohol soon became an addiction, which would escalate over the years.

At first I used alcohol to help with sleep. When my wife and I finally divorced in 1982, I started drinking to suppress any and all of the emotions that had built up in me since 1968. Alcohol was like napalm—it kept the demons at bay. I drank daily—fortunately, most of the time at home. This routine was fine except when someone dropped by or when I needed to go out for an unexpected reason. When I drank in public, I generally embarrassed myself or others with me. I was now a typical alcoholic; I drove while intoxicated, I was aggressive, I fought, I was loud and rude, and I fell down while drunk and passing out in random places. This lifestyle continued into my marriage with my new wife.

Between getting divorced and meeting my new wife, the life I led was a charade. I don't know how I managed it, but I was able to keep alcohol out of the workplace. I can assume this was possible only because I didn't allow anyone in the workplace to get close to me. Another contributing factor to my drinking "success" was the fact that much of my drinking was in private. I taught my classes, worked as a school administrator, and eventually became a university professor. In spite of my alcohol addiction, I was very successful in my profession.

The darker side of my life was a different matter. I'm probably less proud of it than of being alcoholic. It now became my goal to make up for the intimacy I had been deprived of during the time I was trying to put the marriage back together. I became a total womanizer. I had a constant run of short relationships. If I suspected the woman was getting serious, I ended the relationship. Between relationships, I relied on one-night stands to satisfy my needs. Note, I wasn't considering anyone else or her feelings. That didn't seem to matter to me. Later I would look back and feel terribly guilty for the things I had done and the people I had hurt.

I wasn't looking to settle down with anyone. At the end of a summer workshop, the class decided to have a picnic. I took my children with me and met the sister of one of the workshop participants. She was divorced with a six-year-old son. I was very impressed with her and asked her out on a date. Unlike the other relationships I had been in, she was very special. Soon we married, combined our families, and had a daughter of our own. I continued to drink but much less often. There were still too many times when I would drink too much and act in unacceptable ways.

She tolerated my behavior for several years but then made it clear she wasn't going to subject herself and the children to that kind of life. Believe it or not, I stopped drinking overnight. Again, the fear of losing everything wasn't worth the alcohol or what I thought it did for me. I haven't had a drink other than at communion since then. Eighteen years of being sober have convinced me that alcohol wasn't the answer then or now for me or for anyone else suffering from PTSD.

I recognized then that alcohol wasn't the problem but rather an attempted cure or intervention for the real, underlying problem. PTSD symptoms were still a constant presence in my life. The difference now was that I began to realize there was something wrong with me. I wasn't normal and hadn't been since leaving Vietnam.

When I got home in 1968, I'd tried to fool myself by thinking I could attain my pursuit to become normal by achieving my contrived goals. When that failed, I relied on alcohol to mask my symptoms. Now, with a failed marriage behind me, my dreams of a perfect life dashed, and a chance for a good life ahead of me, I had to do something. This process was difficult, because I still didn't know what the real problem was. I had hidden the fact that I was a Vietnam veteran at the workplace. It was all business in the workplace. I didn't want the repercussions that followed my separation from active duty to surface again. I isolated myself from my colleagues and in general kept my military service a secret. I taught my classes, served on committees, published university text, completed my dissertation, and performed all the duties expected of me. The downside of this approach was that I never allowed myself to become close to anyone at work. I taught in two secondary schools and at two large universities without divulging that I had ever been in the military, let alone that I was a Vietnam veteran. When I left a position, I put it behind me and didn't attempt to keep in touch with the colleagues I had worked with.

There was something wrong with me, and I realized I had to find help. I decided to go to my doctor and explain my lengthy periods of depression. I didn't mention anything about Vietnam, because it didn't occur to me at the time that Vietnam had anything to do with my problems. The doctor I chose treated me by prescribing an anxiety medication, which was supposed to stop or reduce the chances of my going into a depression. The meds were to be taken when I started to become anxious. As we all know, at that point it's too late. All the medication accomplished was suppressing my anxiety. In several hours it would return. I tried to control it myself, but without knowing the cause, I wasn't very successful. My control consisted of removing myself from the situation and the people around me. At least I wasn't bothering anyone else, or so I thought, and I wasn't using alcohol.

Being alone didn't remedy the situation, but it did allow me time to collect my emotions and hide them from my family. Emotions are a very difficult thing for me to hide, and to think I was actually successful ended up being an illusion on my part. I hadn't fooled anyone. It was several years later, when facing the real demons, that this fact would become apparent to me. After determining that PTSD was in all probability the root of my problems, I started compiling information for the VA. I asked my sister-in-law, a VA psychiatric nurse at the Brecksville VA hospital, to write a letter on my behalf. Upon reading the letter, I was amazed by how long ago she had realized I had PTSD. Like my family and friends, she'd done nothing for all those years.

In the early 1970s, I was asked to be a charter member of an American Legion post in the city where I was living. I knew the men who were part of it professionally and joined it so they could get the twenty-five members needed to get chartered. It was a small post that did little outside of the community. Even in this veteran organization, I was able to conceal my military background by merely submitting a copy of my DD214 without explanation. It showed that I had separated honorably from the navy, and beyond that nothing was ever talked about. The majority of civilians and a large number of military personnel didn't know what a Seabee was. Least of all did they realize that marines had trained us and that we'd served alongside them while in Vietnam.

I remained a member of the post while teaching at Kent State University in northern Ohio. Upon my retirement in 1998, my family and I moved back to the Newark area. I had the time and decided to reconnect with my comrades in the American Legion post. There were seldom more than six to ten members who would attend meetings or get involved in post activities. In 2000 I was asked to run for commander and accepted the nomination and office. With so few members, I ran unopposed. During my tenure as commander, I did what was expected of me and attended various functions I felt a commander should attend. Those in the local Vietnam Veterans of America (VVA) chapter were hosting their open house, and I felt that as commander of my Legion post, I should attend. After talking for only a few minutes with some of the members, I began to realize these were men I could relate to, and above all they accepted me for who I was. For the first time I felt at ease and somewhat back home. By the time I left

that evening, I had become a member. Now I realize it was actually only my start to returning home.

I felt comfortable in the VVA meetings and
gradually became close to some of my brothers.
Issues such as Agent Orange, veterans' rights, and
PTSD were discussed, to mention a few. During
this time a member of our group recognized
that I had many symptoms of PTSD. He gave me
a booklet and asked me to read it. I did so and
was amazed by the number of similarities between
my problems and the symptoms outlined in the
publication. Reading this booklet prompted me
to start asking more questions about PTSD. Some
of my buddies in the chapter had already been diagnosed with PTSD, and others, like me, were exploring the possibility that they might also have it.
I hadn't actually been diagnosed as having PTSD,
but the similarities between the definitions and my
symptoms were staggering. At this point I basically
diagnosed myself and latched on to buddies in a
similar situation. The bond we formed allowed us
to discuss PTSD and our symptoms openly.

PTSD became a topic small groups of us would
discuss among ourselves and occasionally at the
chapter level. Within several months a few of us
broke off and started having what we called "PTSD
meetings." We had no structure to speak of, but
the meetings gave us a platform to talk about anything we wanted. A brotherhood of trust formed in
this group, allowing us to open up even more. As
time went by, the trust went beyond the meeting.

We became a 24-7 support system for each other. If one of the group members was having a rough time dealing with a problem, he would call another person in the group for help. It was amazing how talking with a trusted buddy could help. To this day we meet twice a month. We are a little more structured now than we were at first. On occasion we have someone speak to us, but our priority is to allow each member to address how he is doing and to raise any topic of concern.

It was during this time that I started attending another PTSD group held at the local VA clinic. A VA nurse/ social worker supervised this group. While a few of the guys from our group attended this, the majority attending this group were new faces to me. Now a fellow veteran and neighbor, who is in my VVA chapter, calls me "the analyzer." I know this title describes my personality accurately, and we laugh about it a lot. When analyzing the VA group, I came to a realization. There are several categories of veterans suffering from PTSD.

One category of veterans doesn't really seek help recovering from it but rather looks for comfort in dealing with it. The comfort they gain comes from meeting in a nonthreatening environment and discussing what is going on in their lives. I don't sense these men really feel there is help out there for them.

While I hate to say it, I believe there is a second group that is more concerned about the percentage of compensation they receive than about actually getting help.

Those in the third group, which comprises the majority of PTSD veterans including myself, just want to find tools to deal with our PTSD issues. We recognize that tools are needed to allow us to better function with our families, in the workplace, and generally in society. We are the veterans who came home with high hopes but over the years recognized that the way we'd approached these hopes and dreams just wasn't right. We couldn't determine what was wrong or, for that matter, what had caused it. Seeking help for PTSD was impossible. How could we seek help for something we hadn't identified? As the years passed, our PTSD symptoms became more and more a part of who we were. In addition to our experiences in Nam, we brought home our PTSD symptoms. These symptoms were never addressed and eventually attached themselves to the young men we had been prior to our service in Vietnam. The layers became so thick that the person beneath couldn't be identified. I relate it to a pie. The thicker the crust, the more difficult it is to identify the filling. This condition led to our being viewed as a collection of symptoms rather than as the persons we actually were. The many problems this situation caused could have easily been eliminated or made less severe if our government, media, civilians, and even veterans from earlier wars would have acknowledged us and the sacrifices we'd made.

Once I recognized I had PTSD, I wanted the VA to acknowledge it. To me this would have at least given a valid explanation for the bizarre behavior I had exhibited for the past thirty-some years. This journey would take me another three years and at many times brought up PTSD symptoms in the process. Had it not have been for my persistence and the support from my PTSD groups, who were helping me through the process, I probably would have given up and become like the first group of veterans I mentioned earlier.

My quest started with a piece of cloth on a metal bar. I am referring to the Combat Action Ribbon (CAR), which I was certain I was entitled to and had earned. My first trip to the Veterans Service Office in Newark confirmed that no stressor was needed if the veteran had earned this ribbon. The veterans service officer assisting me helped fill out my paper work and submitted it to the VA for my PTSD claim. A month or so later, I received a rejection letter from the VA indicating that I hadn't been awarded the CAR. This was a PTSD moment. Now I felt the need for double validation: first, acknowledgment of PTSD; and second, my entitlement for the Combat Action Ribbon. I tried to handle the two situations simultaneously.

The veterans service officer gave me a form to request a DD215, which would reflect all ribbons and medals I was entitled to. I submitted it to military records in St. Louis. Six months later they responded by saying I needed to go through the Department of the Navy in Maryland. I did so. Several months went by before I received notification from them that I had to request the information from St. Louis (another PTSD moment). Although I felt this effort was all in vain, I sent another letter. Approximately four months later I went to the mailbox and found a box containing a DD215 as well as nearly a full set of medals and ribbons, including my Combat Action Ribbon. The very next day I went to the mailbox, and there was another DD215 and another set of medals. Between letters to and letters from, getting the medals I had earned took almost two years.

Meanwhile, through the VSO I had completed another request to be evaluated for PTSD. This time I filled out my stressors. Stressors had to be submitted if you hadn't received either a Combat Infantry Badge (army) or a Combat Action Ribbon (navy or marine corps). Even though I now had my CAR, I was told to follow the stressor procedure. My veterans service officer helped me to complete my rebuttal forms along with a new request to be evaluated. The response, which came several months later, indicated that I should start seeing a VA psychiatrist. My first meeting was very confusing. He talked with me for an hour and concluded by stating that I had held a job, had earned a PhD, and had been a professor at two large universities in Ohio. He admitted that I probably had PTSD but that it didn't appear to have affected my life. I asked him whether I could be evaluated anyway. He saw me two additional times, yet no compensation and pension (C and P) exam was scheduled. On my next visit with him, I asked, "Do I have PTSD?" He turned the computer toward me and in an aggravated voice stated, "See here. It shows that you have PTSD." Still he didn't schedule a C and P. In frustration I went to my veterans service officer and found that I could go to a civilian psychiatrist for a compensation-and-pension evaluation.

I found it beyond my belief that this VA psychiatrist couldn't determine how PTSD had affected my life. He had my post-Vietnam résumé right in front of him. I'll be the first to admit that I had disguised who I was in the workplace. Hell, my colleagues didn't know I was a Vietnam veteran. Had they known, many of my teaching methods would have been condemned. As it was, I was praised for being creative. That is what I faced as a Vietnam veteran. If people knew you were a Nam vet, you were instantly considered half crazy and living on the edge. I found that the best way to function was to hide my Vietnam experiences. This wasn't a difficult task because I wouldn't allow myself to get close to those I worked with. Even at work-related social events, I was reluctant to mix a lot and rarely discussed anything but business.

Whenever I tried to explain how symptoms had affected my private life, the psychiatrist seemed to ignore what I was saying. He explained away my depression as being normal to everyone. For some reason I just couldn't buy into that assessment.

The depression hurt too much, and I hated the effects it had on my family and people I cared about. Consequently, when my veterans service officer told me I could go outside the VA system for an evaluation, I jumped at the chance.

I scheduled an appointment with the county mental health group for an evaluation for PTSD. They administered the PTSD assessment evaluation. When it was complete, the psychiatrist indicated I was rated at fifty-five. At the time all I knew was to take the results to my veterans service officer and that he would submit it through the maze of channels to the VA. I later learned that fifty-five was actually where I fell on the Global Assessment of Functioning scale (GAF). I also learned what this level of functioning actually meant: I had moderate-to-serious PTSD symptoms.

I could go on to define what the charts say about my GAF score, but they didn't really describe me, and I was getting pissed off with charts anyway. It would be easy to pull information from the definitions and point out where I fit between the lines. I resented that anyone could define me in several lines of type. I could pretend to accept the definition, but that would be a lie to myself and a greater disservice to my Vietnam brothers. My PTSD—in fact, the PTSD of my brothers—is unique. It's a type of PTSD that was forged in Vietnam and allowed to simmer for decades. The demons had become part of my life and mind with no outlet other than to display themselves through the symptoms they forced to surface. A psychiatrist or anyone who hasn't walked in my boots has no right to define me by looking at a chart. If he or she could, it would take paragraphs, not lines, to describe the agony my demons put me through.

CHAPTER SEVEN
Battlefield Vietnam:
A Unique War

The Vietnam veteran is unique. The Vietnam War and the way we fought it was unique. Why wouldn't our PTSD be unique? To attempt to answer these questions, you must have served there, returned home from there, and fought—and continue to fight—the demons you brought home from there. If you fall into this category, you will probably understand the following paragraphs.

Why is the Vietnam veteran unique? Why are any of us unique? Maybe I should ask, "What makes us individuals?" Each of us who went to Vietnam took with us not only a duffel bag of gear but also a duffel bag of life experiences. Before becoming soldiers, we were children of parents who'd instilled in us different sets of values. The values our parents taught each of us weren't the same as those the parents of Billy down the street taught him. Different values were emphasized, and each family taught different lessons. Before becoming soldiers, we belonged to different churches—or to no church at all. The doctrines of the churches instilled different beliefs as to how we should conduct our lives. Our demographics differed. We came from cities, towns, villages, and farms. Our economic levels differed but were somewhat consistent; we didn't see many rich kids in the enlisted ranks in Vietnam. The public, movie makers, and authors attempted to clump us together by describing us as generally being blue collar and low middle income to poor, with a high school education or less. Even with that in mind, we were still very different. That difference or individuality in combat is what allowed for different perceptions of the same event. Two soldiers could be side by side, and a traumatic experience could affect one and not the other.

How were the Vietnam War and the way we fought it unique? My perspective may differ slightly from other veterans only because our duties and experiences were different. To start out with a laugh, I'll bet England, France, and Germany didn't smell like burning diesel fuel and shit coupled with rotting fish.

I have viewed almost all movies about Vietnam—one time each. This experience was torture. I believe I subjected myself to them in an effort to find someone out there who understood and validated my service in Vietnam. I also wanted those close to me to be able to view a movie and better understand me and what Vietnam was really like without my having to talk about it. In this way I hoped to be acknowledged, accepted, and possibly understood.

As I try to make my point about Vietnam-focused movies, you will note a great deal of sarcasm in my comments. I'm not suggesting that you should agree with me. Rather, this is my opportunity to point out how I was affected.

You may have seen all or some of the films I'm going to mention. If you haven't, I caution you in advance. I fear they may trigger you as they did me. How were we soldiers depicted in almost all these films?

Apocalypse Now. We were depicted as a bunch of deserting drug heads with no order, control, or mission. The way the brown water navy was depicted was embarrassing. From my limited exposure to the boat crews and ramps they worked out of, I have the deepest respect for these men and their missions.

The Green Berets: This movie was OK, and a number of scenes were accurate. I enjoyed the movie, insomuch that the Seabees were included in a role they so frequently played in Vietnam. You can't say John Wayne didn't love his dirt sailors, the Fighting Seabees. I found it difficult to conceive of the methods used to capture and extract the North Vietnamese Army (NVA) general. Some scenes were believable, but most, in my opinion, were hokey.

The Deer Hunter: What a tragic way for a soldier to meet his end. The background of the typical

Vietnam soldier was accurate. For the most part, we were blue collar and came from middle- to lower-middle-class families. Movie audiences focus on main characters and tend to view an actor's role as being typical of the role the Vietnam soldier played. This fact, coupled with the way the media depicted Vietnam and Vietnam soldiers, was the criterion many Americans used to view us and our war.

Hamburger Hill: How utterly ridiculous that one was. However, it was probably accurate when you consider how many men were lost acquiring an objective that had no strategic purpose and was occupied only for a very brief time. All Vietnam veterans could relate to that tactic.

Full Metal Jacket: Boot camp was shown realistically with only a few exceptions. My gunny sergeant in boot would have probably castrated the Joker on the pretense that he didn't want him to reproduce. Leonard's mental problems would have been recognized, and he would have been removed from his training company. I could accept the Battle for Hue City to some extent except for the grand march out at the end of the movie. I can attest that we didn't exit that hellhole singing the theme song to the *Mickey Mouse Club*.

We Were Soldiers: The only thing one could have concluded from this film was that the lessons learned there weren't applied to the rest of the war. It portrayed the First Air Cavalry engagement with a large force of the NVA at the Battle of Ia Drang

Valley in 1965. Our enemy was smart, resourceful, dedicated, and wise to combat.

Platoon: This movie was full of cowardice, drugs, prejudice, and dishonor. Why do the writers and producers always seem to emphasize the negative aspects of the Vietnam War and the men who fought it? What a distortion of the truth and a disservice to those of us who fought there, not to mention those who gave their lives there.

The World War II films we grew up on were entirely different. Not that they didn't show drama, death, and destruction, but in the end you always had a hero and some form of victory. The sad thing about Vietnam films was that I always came away feeling ashamed, embarrassed, hurt, and triggered. I viewed them seeking validation and ended up feeling depressed. What we all wanted was validation and acceptance for our service. In the end we could be validated only by each other. The films I mentioned didn't emphasize how unique Vietnam really was. Come to think of it, there weren't many producers on my section of perimeter or behind my transit at the Perfume River during Tet.

It took a very short amount of time for me to realize that I had little, if any, reason to be in Vietnam. Thus, I did my job, put in my time, and prayed for my short-timer's calendar to run out of spaces. During that time all I really thought was, I gotta get out of this place, as the lyrics to the song went. The only exceptions were taking care of my buddies and relying on them to take care of me.

I spent the majority of my time trying to stay sane in an insane place. I seemed to be living in a constant struggle between opposites: boredom and adrenaline rush. This dichotomy wasn't good for my mental stability.

The Vietnamese people led a simple life and for the most part just wanted to be left alone to pursue it. Our presence there and the American dollar picked up where the French had left off in screwing up a culture that had existed thousands of years before our arrival. Why try to fix something that's not broken? The average Vietnamese was forced to become a traitor. Our general approach was to occupy the villages by day and then go back to our base camps or fire bases at night. This routine gave Charlie (VC) the villages at night. Since the need for survival is man's strongest need, the villagers had to accept us during the day and the Vietcong, or VC, after sundown. This situation presented a conflict to us as well. We weren't sure who was friend and who was enemy. Not knowing which straw hat the Vietnamese was wearing made each encounter potentially volatile. Once we experienced this problem firsthand, it wasn't usually long into our tour that we became skeptical of the Vietnamese people. Trust was the big issue, and where the Vietnamese people were concerned, we had little or none. We liked the children and felt sorry for them, but for the most part, we detested the parents. You fed the kids C rations and destroyed their parents' crops. My conscious and subconscious mind had difficulty understanding this concept. Trying to understand anything that went on in Vietnam was a waste of time.

My battalion didn't permit Vietnamese to be in our base camp perimeter. However, in the spring of 1967 in Chu Lai, our battalion was doing an inventory of our supply yard. To hasten the process, Vietnamese workers were allowed in camp to assist. They were there two days. The next night after they were done, we came under a heavy mortar attack, which resulted in three KIAs (killed in action) and nine wounded. Another opposite: we exchanged our money and food for mortars.

Following the Tet Offensive in 1968, the 101st Airborne Division moved just east of our combat base. On some nights we were on our bunkers, drinking a beer and watching a firefight or mortar attack taking place at Camp Eagle. Several days later they would be watching us go through the same thing. It seemed insane to take ground and give it back, build something by day and know it would probably be destroyed that night, befriend a Vietnamese by day and feel he would try to kill you by night. These factors, in my opinion, made the whole war senseless. Even more senseless was the fact that we had to be there. We had been converted from believing we were fighting communism to the reality that our war was fighting politicians.

Life was either low key and you were bored out of your mind, or your adrenaline was so high, you felt like your mind was going to explode. There

didn't seem to be much in between. A Seabee battalion was a little different, at least from a surveyor's
standpoint. We were on jobsites most of the time,
which didn't allow for much boredom. However,
any free time was boredom time. It seemed like we
were always going from one side of the spectrum
to the other. When I look back, I really feel sorry
for those officers who were our direct leaders. An
enlisted man was allowed to be bored. We could
find a number of ways to somewhat relieve that
boredom. I won't go into detail, but these ways
were many and frequently very bizarre.

Officers were not afforded that luxury. Most
of the time officers had to pretend not to be affected by the things enlisted men complained
about. Most enlisted men saw the several-year age
difference as making the officer immune to what
affected him. The first-line officers were no different from foremen on the factory floor. Their superiors gave them little respect because they were
too close to their men, and most men felt officers
were just part of management. Some officers were
able to walk the tightrope and come away from
Vietnam unaffected. Others brought home the
demons of combat as well as the demons of command. Command demons, like all PTSD demons,
are not understood by civilians. Hell, most enlisted
men don't understand them.

All branches and units were provided gear and
equipment based on some Washington-contrived
hierarchy of wants or needs. Don't try to figure it

out, or you will be driven as crazy as those who created the priority list. It didn't make sense to me then or now. But as an enlisted man, I probably wasn't considered capable of understanding. As I perceived it, the trickle-down effect went this way: air force, blue water navy, army, brown water navy, marines, and finally Seabees. There were exceptions, but in general, this is the way it went. How crazy was the concept? If a Seabee wanted jungle greens, he had to trade for them. I procured my flak jacket as payment for a debt a cook owed me. I loaned him $200 while he was shooting craps. He lost and had to pay me with his flak jacket. You did what you had to do to make an already-miserable life a little easier or a little safer.

I don't believe this was a Seabees problem alone. Many small units and units performing missions or assignments outside the unit's military definition also faced similar situations. Comfort is one thing, but military gear and equipment are something else. On my second tour, which included the Battle for Hue City, I didn't have a bayonet for my M16. When I separated from duty four months later, you could buy one in an army/navy store in San Francisco. For that matter I didn't get an M16 until July of 1967. Throughout my second tour, I was the only member in my squad issued hand grenades. You may ask why. I was instructed to use them to destroy the three M60s in my squad if we were being overrun. Why not issue them to all my squad and try to save the guns? In my little corner of the war, these practices seemed not only unique but also stupid. Thank God for the marines! They kept us well supplied with the armaments we needed. This fact may not be appropriate, but we kept the marines well supplied with beer.

Somewhere up the ranks a major screw-up had been made—we always had beer, lots and lots of beer. It wasn't clear why Seabees were entitled to this beer allotment, but beer was our currency in Vietnam. Marines loved us, and other branches tolerated us for our beer. Our beer allotment allowed us to procure needed items (as well as many we didn't technically need). Very probably these situations, events, or practices were typical of other wars; however, Vietnam was *our* war, and typical or not, they impacted us.

One thing I'm sure of is that the society we came home to was anything but typical of other wars. If you were a Vietnam veteran, you felt like a marked man. It was bad enough that you brought the demons home, but now you also had to fight or hide from the society you had been fighting for. We were viewed as weird Vietnam veterans. People feared us, avoided us, and talked about us but made no effort to understand us or help us fight our demons. Let me give a personal example.

My wife and I were married in her parents' home. Her family, my children, and a few friends, including my service buddy from New York, were the only ones who attended. Following the brief ceremony, my father-in-law and my buddy went to the back porch to have a smoke. One brother-in-law followed them to the porch. As they were making small talk, my new brother-in-law commented, "I worry about Patty getting married to that Vietnam vet because they're not very stable." Little did he know that the guy beside him had spent two tours with that Vietnam vet. My buddy didn't tell me for several years. When he did, he indicated that if it hadn't been for the wedding, he would have made my new sister-in-law a widow.

How could anyone think our PTSD wouldn't be uniquely ours? I'm convinced that the PTSD symptoms I suffered, and continue to suffer, wouldn't have been as severe or possibly wouldn't have manifested themselves at all if our government and society in general hadn't treated me differently upon my return from Vietnam.

The current consensus seems to be that the sooner you're treated after a traumatic event, the less likely you are to have prolonged PTSD symptoms. At least the severity of the symptoms would be less. This is a wonderful finding, and it's great to see it applied to survivors of school shootings, rapes, muggings, and so forth. But what had happened when it came to Vietnam veterans? Our government didn't want to acknowledge that the traumatic events we'd experienced had any adverse effect on us at all. Any treatment we received was something we had to solicit and then fight for to receive. The delay of several decades, accompanied by the bureaucracy we had to fight, created more triggers and more severe symptoms. These factors enhanced even more that we weren't acknowledged for our sacrifice. To most Vietnam veterans, we needed that acknowledgment more than anything else.

Describing society as a single entity is unfair. Individuals make up society, and at the time each person had his or her own beliefs and feelings regarding Vietnam. Various groups, organizations, and geographic areas also had specific beliefs about the war. But in general, voicing negative opinions about the war and Vietnam veterans had become more acceptable. The media was certainly willing to capitalize on that trend. Society neither knew nor understood the impact this negativity had on the Vietnam vet. The open controversies regarding Vietnam only heightened the frequency of intrusive thoughts and triggers for the veteran.

Vietnam veterans were not very trusting of the government, but they were extremely loyal to the country. They viewed antiwar, antigovernment demonstrations, for the most part, as being organized and attended by individuals who were less than patriotic. These events and the exploitation of the events by Hollywood and the media provided more triggers for the Vietnam veteran. We had learned the difference between dissention and patriotism. We had learned the difference between dissention and loyalty. We had learned the difference between dissention and duty.

CHAPTER EIGHT
Search and Destroy:
Attacking PTSD

Once the county mental health agency confirmed that I had PTSD, I was confident that the VA would have to accept its findings and acknowledge my condition. The Department of Defense had taken nearly two years to acknowledge the medals I had earned. Consequently, I knew it would take an act of God for the VA to act any faster. No surprises there! Almost three years passed before they finally awarded my claim.

The following paragraphs are nothing more than the road map I followed in my effort to attack PTSD. I call it a road map because when I look back, a very defined order of events took place. I believe a veteran who can follow the same road map will also find it to be beneficial. I have to be extremely careful to get the sequence of events in the proper order and provide all the details in a manner that will make it easily understood. To

105

succeed in this effort, I need to focus on you and make suggestions for you. The suggestions I make are the approaches that have worked for me. They may or may not work for everyone, but trying them won't hurt. Trying anything is better than doing nothing. I stated earlier that my journey home from PTSD has taken at least ten years since I first realized I had PTSD. I also recognize now that there is no final destination—only a number of more pleasant stops along the way.

The most difficult part of the journey home for the Vietnam veteran is identifying whether he has PTSD. This task is nearly impossible without help from fellow veterans, and the most helpful veterans are those who have already recognized the symptoms in themselves and identified trust as the key element that helped. They also believe trust is the key to helping other vets. A certain level of trust already exists between Vietnam veterans. It's this trust that will make us more receptive to listening and understanding what another Nam vet points out.

Convincing a brother that he may have PTSD can be a long and exhausting process. While there are many successes, each resulting in a most rewarding experience, not all attempts end this way. Some veterans seem happy to live in their world of doom and gloom; it's almost like they embrace their PTSD symptoms. Some even seem proud of their symptoms, and others seem to be afraid to unleash the demons. While I do understand how they feel, these brothers will continue to live with their demons. Still others, like my best friend, Gary, refuse to recognize anything is wrong with them. These veterans blame their lot in life on others, generally view the glass as half empty, and have difficulty retaining friends or forming relationships.

For veterans who are reached, like me, however, the world starts to become a better place. In turn we become advocates in bringing home more brothers with PTSD. I don't know how I can ever thank enough those Vietnam buddies who helped me.

After I became aware that I showed many signs of PTSD, the monkey was on my back. No one ever told me that living with, or recovering from, PTSD was easy. First, I had to resign myself to the fact that getting relief included initial pain. Not only did I have to deal with my demons; I now faced the guilt of having hurt and inflicted pain on others. In many cases I didn't realize my actions had hurt others; nevertheless they had. Once that can of worms was open, I had to prepare myself to face the many people I had hurt over the decades since leaving Vietnam. It was bad enough facing myself but even more devastating facing those around me. I had a very difficult time admitting that I had to take responsibility for the damage I had done both to relationships and to my loved ones' lives.

But I had to get used to it. While PTSD had made my life miserable, it likewise had made my loved ones' lives miserable as well. What made the situation worse was that PTSD had haunted me for all those years without my even realizing it. As I struggled through this phase of recovery, I had to keep in close contact with my Vietnam buddies, the buddies who had initially helped me identify my problems. Remember, they had gone through this phase and were willing and able to help me through it. I mentioned earlier that helping someone is like getting a wounded buddy to an aid station or medevac chopper; you do what needs to be done and thank God for the opportunity he gave you to do it. My buddies were there to help me, and never once did I sense they begrudged that help. As I accumulated tools to deal with PTSD, I found that helping a brother is a tool in itself. It soon became apparent to me that allowing a brother to help me was actually helping him also.

When I realized the need for acquiring additional tools to deal with my symptoms, I became more connected with my local Veterans Service Office and the VA. My veterans service officer was aware of all the available help I needed. He arranged an appointment for me at the VA clinic in Columbus. I met with a VA psychiatrist, who initially just talked with me and set up additional appointments. The job of a VA psychiatrist is primarily to evaluate and prescribe medications. I actually thought they would analyze my symptoms and work through them with me. As a result, I became frustrated and triggered due to my early experiences with VA psychiatrists. Like most veterans who suffer from PTSD, I was prescribed medication. I didn't let this scare me, because I knew I needed something extra to help me face the demons that had been hiding for so many years. I recognized that this part of my journey home would be a very difficult one, and I needed all the help I could get.

I find it sad that many of my brothers are unable to move beyond this point. Some stop and go back to their old habits. Others stop and view their journey as complete. It is unfortunate for them that they can't, or won't, struggle through the stages of recovery that will contribute to a much happier life. The soldiers willing to fight the PTSD battle find that subsequent stages become easier and easier. There are setbacks along the way, but each setback becomes less difficult to deal with. The setbacks (triggers and reactions) are like snipers: they have to be taken out one at a time. Tools are like weapons in the arsenal. The more you have, the better are your odds at defeating the enemy. If you persist, your life will improve.

Throughout the recovery process, I had to stay close to my Vietnam buddies. I encountered times when I would regress. My buddies always provided me with an outlet and support mechanism. I consider my buddies to be the first and most versatile tool in my recovery toolbox. I try very hard to be the kind of friend and buddy to other Vietnam veterans and younger combat veterans that these men have been to me.

To take this one step further, I found that being able to bond with one, possibly two, buddies made the fear of dealing with PTSD and the demons a lot easier to handle. I didn't seek out an alliance of this type, and I'm not suggesting anyone does. This kind of bond between brothers has to happen naturally. If there is a formula for this, I don't know it. What I do know is that bonding helped me. When I started forming these bonds, a great number of my inhibitions disappeared. I wasn't afraid to call these guys day or night for fear of bothering them. I wasn't afraid to ask for help. Most importantly, I found buddies I trusted and felt comfortable talking with. I had gone years without that luxury.

I'm fortunate to have paired up with several such buddies. Neither I nor they are reluctant to share our demons with each other, seek help from each other, or just listen to each other. I believe this comradeship provides a security blanket I desperately needed. It was such a relief just knowing there was someone there if I needed help or if a demon appeared. These guys also know I'm there for them. The relationship I have with these men has allowed me to be more receptive to allowing others into my circle of trust. I recognize there may be others who feel comfortable and trust me. I may be the Nam vet who helps them identify and battle their demons. I can't screw up this mission.

Like the majority of Vietnam veterans, I'm very perceptive. This quality may have evolved from the hypervigilance needed for survival in Vietnam. Perception, in my opinion, is very similar to hyper-vigilance but relates more to people than to surroundings. I have found this trait to be extremely helpful when dealing with other Vietnam veterans. I feel like I can sense if one of my buddies is having a rough time. When this happens, I don't hesitate to be there for him. The trigger may not be clear to me, and I don't need to hear the story. Often a story isn't necessary unless the vet wants to share it. Just knowing that I'm there and care will generally relieve his anxiety. When his anxiety level lessens, he will have time to think out and better handle his situation. I don't try to analyze his trigger or story—being a good listener is what he needs. Using my perception in this way has enabled me to be a better positive influence to other Vietnam veterans I come in contact with.

Keeping in close contact with my Vietnam buddies was essential as I continued my journey home. As I become more and more comfortable, seeking more involvement with other veterans became important for me. I began exploring vet-eran organizations in my area. I talked with other Nam vets who were members of various veteran organizations, and if the organizations sounded good, I tried them out. I didn't continue attending meetings with some of them, and I knew member-ship could always be dropped. For others I really enjoyed the meetings and welcomed the chance to make new veteran friends as well. If I believed the organization shared a similar philosophy with mine, I gradually got more involved in it.

Most veteran groups are active in a number of ways. Being involved in every event or activity wasn't necessary. I tried to pick the events I was interested in and felt I could contribute to. What should raise the red flag is the number of events and the amount of your involvement. I began spending more and more time away from my family. Most of my life had been spent away from them either physically or mentally. I was abandoning them again, but this time I was too involved in my organizations. My family had waited years for the real me to be part of their lives; I had to be careful not to let them down again. I couldn't neglect them now by letting veteran activities take over my life. Just as my family was part of my life with PTSD, they needed to be part of my life as I recovered from it.

Once I became involved with the VA and connected with a psychiatrist, I was made aware of social workers and small groups of veterans who were also dealing with PTSD symptoms. Attending these meetings can be very difficult as well as potentially very beneficial. I was comfortable in some groups and uncomfortable in others. I felt comfortable in some meetings and uncomfortable in others. In some meetings what was said or the actions of an attending member or a small group attending the meeting actually triggered me. Sometimes the dynamics of the group didn't seem to fit my needs, and if I wasn't feeling that any personal gains were being made, then I concluded that the group wasn't right for me.

Some groups I attended were composed of veterans who were stuck where they were and couldn't make progress beyond that point. I'm not being critical of these vets. They probably have reached their individual plateaus. They have each other, a benefit that provides them with comradeship and a reason for living. These groups had a tendency to pull me down more than to offer me help. I felt like I could go further with my recovery, and I didn't want to settle for a group that was happy with the status quo. After feeling alone for decades with my purposes in life that were contrived and irrational, acceptance by a group was progress in itself. My mind was fragile, and I grasped for anything that relieved the pain of isolation and the solitary confinement I had learned to accept. For these reasons I couldn't allow myself to accept some groups. Several times I nearly allowed myself to fall into the trap of adaptation. Adaptation may have appeared to be progress, and to a degree it was. It wasn't enough for me. Once I made this much progress, I felt as though I could go further and set higher recovery goals for myself.

If the desire for comradeship is something you want and need, yet you feel uncomfortable with the groups in the VA or veterans center, there is another option. You may have already bonded with fellow veterans you *do* feel comfortable with. Talk to these men. There is a possibility that together you can form a small group of your own. This formation isn't as simple as it may sound. People, gatherings, or groups will initially be somewhat fluid. Veterans will come and go at first, but in the end you will probably have a core group of people who share the same type of comradeship you're looking for. We are all different, and some veterans feel more comfortable with one-on-one relationships. Others seek out veterans with similar experiences in Nam or after their return from Nam. Some veterans just feel more secure in a group setting. Many like to share their day-to-day activities, while others like to deal more with their PTSD symptoms.

Your needs may vary, but be assured that they *can* be met. Meeting with your brothers in a group, gathering for breakfast or lunch, or even attending a veterans organization meeting may satisfy your need for comradeship. Frequently, all it takes is a telephone call to a trusted buddy to provide the needed comradeship or to defuse a triggered emotion. Whatever you decide, make sure it is helpful to you. Remember, during the healing process, we are very fragile, and your needs may change at any time. Triggers are always present in our lives and will be present throughout our lives. To keep on the path to recovery, you may need one-on-one time with a close buddy. There may be times you need a small group or a gathering of a few buddies. There may be times when you want only comradeship and companionship. There may be other times when you need to focus on more serious topics related to your recovery. There may also be times when you feel like you just need to listen.

Having Vietnam veteran comrades is essential. At some point you will need to attack the demons. I believe this can be achieved only by having a close relationship with your brothers. They too have demons to attack, and like in Vietnam, having a trusted buddy by your side and covering your back are always best.

For years we have allowed the demons to manipulate and dominate our lives. It's time we go on the offensive and take back some lost ground. Don't get pinned down by giving up! Don't get pinned down by feeling sorry for yourself or by wallowing in self-pity, anger, and resentment. Do something about your problem. Use whatever it takes to find tools that allow you to engage and win battles against the demons.

CHAPTER NINE
Cans on the Wire: Triggers and Depression

Demons are my PTSD symptoms. I have lived with and fought them since leaving Vietnam. I can battle them, but to win or gain ground, I first had to know the enemy. I don't believe the demons appear as a symptom in themselves. For thirty years I had come face-to-face with my PTSD symptoms, and for another decade I struggled to understand them. Even though my knowledge is limited, I have come to understand myself and get a better handle on how PTSD affects me. I now realize that in my case a PTSD symptom is a complex set of events that take place in a very orderly manner. I first get triggered; I react to the trigger, followed by guilt for my reaction; and finally, I go into depression.

All of us who suffer from PTSD are predisposed to react or overreact to any number of events. The events and our reactions to them are veteran

specific. We all have our own demons, and consequently, our reactions to them are very individual.
Regardless of the difference, our personal demons
set us up to overreact. For the sake of consistency
with PTSD terminology, I will call these events
"triggers."

A world without triggers would be a world
of normality and peace for the Vietnam veteran
suffering from PTSD. The more I think about
it, would there even be PTSD without triggers?
Unfortunately, we veterans didn't come home to
a world void of triggers. They can present themselves in so many different ways, and the ways are
as diverse as Vietnam vets. Triggers are the first
element of a PTSD symptom. They are followed by
our actions or reactions after the trigger.

Triggers appear to the veteran in many forms.
Some are the result of something that originated
in his mind. These would include, but are not limited to, intrusive thoughts, dreams, nightmares,
and flashbacks. Others are environmental—for
example, walking a trail in the woods, being in a
crowd, having to sit in a certain seat, or sensing
insecurity in any way. Our senses open us up to
any number of triggers. Sounds (or a lack thereof)
are as contributive as a scent or certain smells. The
hypervigilance we had to practice in Nam honed
our sense of movement around us, and the sense
of touch also affects us in the form of wet feet or
clothing, pouring rain, dry dust and mud, and—
last but not least—the sixth sense. For me the sixth

sense comprises all my senses acting on full alert at the same time. Our minds combine the data gathered from all our senses. This collection of data allows us to predict an event with a higher-than-average rate of accuracy. The more frequently we predict accurately, the more we rely on our sixth sense.

People probably present us with more triggers than all other sources combined. When we face triggers initiated by people, it's up to us to react to, avoid, ignore, or learn to accept them. We must remember that unless we have been there, true understanding is impossible. Many people try to understand, and some think they do understand. Their lack of knowledge or understanding, however, frequently triggers us without their being aware that they are doing so. I will briefly mention a tool my good Vietnam buddy introduced to me. He shared with me that when this lack of knowledge or understanding in others occurs, he steps back and says to himself, It's not their fault. This tool has proved very valuable to me in reducing potential triggers.

Most people don't *try* to trigger us—it's our *perception* of what they say or do that presents the problem. To those individuals who purposely try to pull the trigger, I can only say, "Watch out." A Vietnam veteran with PTSD isn't a good person to back into a corner or hit cold with something. Though I have gotten considerably better, I haven't been able to handle that behavior yet. The people we live with and love are subject to our overreactions more than anyone else. These are the people to whom we have subjected our symptoms to for years. It's these loved ones we owe our recovery to.

Until the Vietnam veteran with PTSD learns tools to deal with his symptoms, his reactions and overreactions to triggers will be instant and, in many cases, extreme. The ability to react quickly in Vietnam was an asset to his survival and to the survival of the men around him. The veteran first trained in and then practiced the art of quick response. Reaction replaced the idea of first thinking about a situation. Unfortunately, this scenario doesn't work well in a civilian setting.

When we are confronted with a trigger and react, how we react is our choice. The key here is to buy enough time to make a choice. The type of trigger will bring about different responses from different veterans. Our reactions to triggers are generally referred to as our PTSD symptoms. I would like to compare a PTSD symptom to a hand grenade. When we were in Vietnam, a grenade wasn't available to us if it was in the armory. However, today we carry the symptom with us just as we once held a hand grenade. The trigger is literally pulling the pin and releasing the spoon. The exploding grenade is compared to our reaction to the trigger. If you can relate to this comparison, it becomes easy to accept that the trigger and reaction are the key elements that make up a PTSD symptom.

Depending on the trigger, we may elect to fight, flee, or submit. In any case we can trust that not much thought, if any, was given to our reaction. This truth leads to a very important part of learning to live with PTSD. Tools are needed that will buy us time between the trigger and our reaction to it. If we're given enough time to rationalize or think before we act, our choices will likely be much more acceptable both to those around us and ultimately to ourselves. If we can control our reactions, we can avoid many of the consequences for bad actions. We must constantly remind ourselves that triggers and the way we react to triggers are what get us into trouble. Apparently the easy solution would be to avoid triggers and not react to them when they do occur. This tactic, however, is much easier said than done. Our reactions may appear to be a single PTSD symptom. While these reactions may be the first symptom, we must realize that they set the stage for follow-up symptoms, such as isolation, depression, and anger.

Recognizing what PTSD is and how complex it can become is important. PTSD is a diagnosis for a number of symptoms a person can exhibit. You can't put your hand on PTSD, and at times putting your hand on a symptom is difficult. *Symptom* is an intangible word that doesn't become tangible until its elements or reactions to it surface. Without the tangible elements of the symptom, there would be no symptom. With this understanding we can recognize that attacking a symptom is impossible.

If a veteran attempts to do so, he may wind up pissing in the wind and getting sprinkled with failure. The only way I can work on a symptom is to break it down to the responses I exhibit. While many of us may have the same symptom, it likely won't surface in the same way or be brought on by the same trigger.

A veteran's reaction to a trigger may appear to be the only element of the symptom he needs to deal with. But in actuality he needs tools to help him deal with them all. Reactions are somewhat easy to identify and analyze. Triggers aren't that simple. They vary greatly. Some happen quickly and can be identified just as quickly. Other triggers develop slowly, making the veteran vulnerable to imagined triggers that gets coupled with the initial trigger. The more complex a trigger becomes, the more difficult it is to identify and deal with. Triggers and reactions are veteran specific; those things that trigger us and how we react to them are specific to the individual veteran. Symptoms, on the other hand, can easily be defined and tend to be common to all of us. By recognizing this fact, we can share tools and use them to fight the elements of common symptoms.

As a specific Vietnam veteran, I want to use my symptoms, reactions, and triggers as an example. The end result of any reaction to a trigger is guilt. Guilt due to my reaction always throws me into a depressed state. This was my signature end result long before I was aware that I had PTSD. That

I was aware of the sequence but unaware of the cause is ironic. Until I recognized my PTSD and learned some tools to deal with the symptoms, I reacted to triggers without considering the impact my reaction had on myself and those around me. My reactions were rarely, if ever, acceptable. Guilt followed when I sobered up or when someone confronted me about what I had done.

I hadn't wanted to overreact, and I certainly hadn't wanted to hurt those around me. Since this wasn't what I desired, guilt overwhelmed me. I didn't actually think of suicide as we know it. I just wanted to run away. I didn't feel that my loved ones deserved to have to deal with me or my problems. I believed that I wasn't worthy of them and that they would be better off without my being around. Thank God, I just couldn't do it. Another guilty feeling was introduced. Now I felt guilty because I was too selfish to leave and relieve their pain and suffering. Depression accompanied this obtuse train of thought.

After I became aware of PTSD and how it affected me, I realized that not all veterans approached this stage the same way. Some actually took the suicide approach. One of the men in my squad committed suicide soon after his return from Nam. Some committed suicide using alcohol or drugs. The death may have been slower, but it was death just the same.

My observation is that some veterans never actually leave the reaction stage. They get triggered and go into the reaction or overreaction mode. Their triggers are almost constant; consequently, they stay in a state of reaction. I had a great deal of difficulty understanding how anyone could stay in that state. When I reacted to a trigger, I was out of control. I hated being out of control and couldn't imagine staying in that state. The whole concept really confused me until I was able to understand it. It was very simple. When I'm in reaction mode, I'm totally out of control and on automatic pilot. The ironic truth is that I think I'm in total control. Once I figured this situation out, it was clear how my brothers could get stuck here. It almost seems like the vets who can't get out of this mode have accepted it as their normal state and feel comfortable in it. Maybe they are comfortable there, although I can't imagine it. The other two options that come to mind are these: either they have no reason or desire to break out of that state, or they don't possess the tools to help them break out. I know how much I need tools to help me, and I suspect that lack of tools is the primary reason other veterans have difficulty getting out of their ruts.

While the lack of tools may be to blame, another possibility exists. Earlier I pointed out that more than anything we veterans want to be acknowledged and accepted. Quite possibly, veterans who don't have the desire to improve their life, have found a negative form of acknowledgment in staying where they are. I can't say their choice is highly accepted, but compared to those of us who work at attaining a better life, it is easier.

Lack of tools is a primary cause contributing to veterans going from reaction mode into developing other symptoms. These veterans are on the same automatic pilot I experienced. The subconscious plays funny tricks, and to the veteran suffering from PTSD, the tricks aren't so funny. There are a number of thoughts hidden in veterans' minds that may cause them to go right into other symptoms following their triggered reactions. The way each of us deals with PTSD is so varied and results from so many variables acting on us that anyone presuming to know all the answers is a fraud. We should all know that trying to figure ourselves out is challenging enough. Most of us living with PTSD know we can't do this without help.

Depression isn't a state of being that affects only the Vietnam veteran. However, for the civilian the cause is usually identifiable. I concede that, like us, some civilians who suffer from depression may not know its origin. The Vietnam veteran suffering from PTSD rarely knows where the depression comes from. There is one saving grace. The more knowledge gained about your PTSD and the more tools you learn to use to combat it, the less severe depression will become.

The depression event also solicits reactions from the vet. The most severe reaction is suicide, as I mentioned briefly. In most suicide cases it is an obvious conclusion. What most people don't realize is that there are many more cases of suicide that no one recognizes. If they aren't recognized as suicide, then it is impossible for me to know for sure. However, most Vietnam veterans know of one or more Nam vets who were in vehicle or motorcycle accidents and where they have lost their life. Generally alcohol is designated as the cause. Are they sure? How many of these accidents are single-vehicle tragedies with no one else involved?

Personally I had a friend I worked with before we both went to Vietnam. While he was gone, his wife left him. Upon his return he was devastated. Several weeks after returning home, he was driving at a very high rate of speed and crashed into a concrete barrier. I have always thought his death was a suicide. There are less violent forms of suicide, such as drug overdoses (with drugs prescribed or not). An even lesser form is abuse of alcohol or drugs to the point that the veteran brings on his own death and, on occasion, the death of others. If the veteran doesn't die through driving drunk, this form of substance abuse can put the veteran in a situation or environment that, in itself, is unsafe and potentially life threatening.

Loneliness frequently accompanies depression. I'm not sure about the psychological reasons, but when I suffer depression, the feeling of loneliness is always present. I believe I bring this feeling on myself, probably because I don't believe anyone will understand or be able to help me. The possibility exists that I'm just feeling sorry for myself. There is one exception to this rule. A fellow Vietnam veteran may help bring me out of it, and a close buddy is the best. When I started to recover from PTSD, I found that having a fellow veteran I could trust and count on to be there for me was necessary.

Isolation is closely related to loneliness or the feeling of wanting to be alone. Generally when I suffer from depression, my only thought is to get away from everyone. This thought manifests in different ways depending on the severity of the depression. With severe depression, I want to hide in a secluded spot. All energy seems to be drained from my body. I'm almost in a vegetative state with no desire to do anything. When I'm like this, I find that working myself out of depression is very difficult. In less severe cases, I can get away and become isolated in a more comfortable environment. The typical spots are usually in a garage, in a workshop, on a lake, in the woods, or in a car or on a motorcycle while driving.

Another type of isolation comes in the form of non-communication. While in a depressed state, I don't generally want conversation. During this time it seems like everyone wants to know what is wrong. This desire only sets me off more, because I can't always explain the reason. I know others can't help when we may not understand the cause ourselves. Sometimes I wonder where they were before I went into the depression. When I'm in a depressed state, I don't really suspect most people care anyway. I emphasize that these thoughts occur during my depression. Once again, if anyone can help by talking, it's a buddy.

I would like to think I try to hide my depression from those around me. But down deep, I believe I want everyone to recognize that something is depressing me. By showing my depression overtly, I can share my pain and hurt with those around me, making their lives as miserable as mine. I'm embarrassed to admit that I've actually acted this way. It's not who I am, and void of PTSD, you probably wouldn't find me moping around, staring off into the distance, and literally not talking to anyone. My other approach is to be an ass to those around me. In this instance I slam things around, mutter to myself, and utter profanities under my breath. All the time I want both sympathy for, and relief from, my pain. The only way to get those is to bring people down to my level. It's almost like we want company in our misery.

The majority of the time I seclude myself and try to figure a way out of the depression on my own. I would like to think depression can be hidden. Who do I think I'm kidding? Depression is like a cold that spreads to all those we come into contact with. When I do try to hide depression, I'm kidding myself into thinking that my friends and family don't recognize my emotions and actions. They may not understand the reason or be able to offer me help, but believe me, they know the effects.

Since I have become more knowledgeable of PTSD and the way it has affected me, I sincerely believe a veteran who has neither recognized he has PTSD nor attempted to get help is always depressed to some degree. He may feel like he's doing fine, but depression is always lurking in the shadows of his mind. If that is true, how does he get the times when he doesn't feel depressed?

One method I tried with little success was looking forward to an event or experience. Frequently, I would create the ideal experience to become involved in. In my mind I imagined the event to go perfectly. I should have known better. How many events in my life have ever gone perfectly? If something went wrong, I would end up even more depressed.

Another common approach for me was to buy myself out of depression. Usually the item or items I bought were frivolous and not in the budget. In a way I felt like I deserved them in addition to their making me feel less depressed. For a brief time my depression was relieved. But within a day or two, I became more depressed as I recognized how ridiculous the purchase was. Sometimes after an extended period of depression, I gradually came out of it on my own. I'm sure there are reasons why I'm able to do this, but I can't identify them. Being depressed made me feel guilty. I knew it hurt those around me, forcing me to tough it out and accept the causes. For whatever reason, after several weeks I would work myself out of it. Earlier

I stated that I will never be rid of PTSD. Learning tools to use to deal with the symptoms and putting them into practice are my salvation.

Just recently I found myself in a situation that put that theory to the test. I believe it will add credibility to many things I have said. For the past several weeks, I dealt dealing with the possibility of losing my Chesapeake Bay retriever to a blood disorder. I trained her from a pup, and I couldn't ask for a better companion and hunting partner. On top of that, she is a family dog whom our children and grandchildren love. She is holding her own, and recovery is hopeful, but she is still in critical condition and possibly won't have a long-term recovery. The whole situation presented me with a gigantic trigger. I dealt with potentially losing her and accepted that her recovery was out of my control. Initially, I felt like I was letting both her and the family down, because I couldn't be counted on to save her. I suspect that all this made me vulnerable to the second part of the depression that followed.

I was able to keep my composure when dealing with the potential loss of my hunting companion. However, I was still worried about her, and my tolerance to fight depression had been weakened. My buddy called and asked whether I thought we could include our wives or partners in some of our group meetings. I suggested that we take our wives to dinner that evening and discuss the matter with them. If I would have had any idea of the impact the meeting would have on me, I never would have suggested it. My wife shared things I had done or how I had acted during the years when my PTSD was at its peak and I was dependent on alcohol as my intervention of choice. My reaction was to become instantly quiet and angry with my wife. My buddy and his wife hadn't known me then, and I imagine I wasn't ready to share that dark side of my life with them just yet. I was embarrassed and felt bad that my buddy's wife had to hear what I had been like. She, in turn, indicated that she had seen my anger in a meeting we had both attended. She brought up that a number of people feared me. I hate that anyone fears me. I don't want to be thought of in that way, and the statement put me into an instant depression. In addition, I actually couldn't remember most of the things my wife said I had done. That didn't surprise me since I had probably been intoxicated at the time. I was embarrassed that the conversation had come up at all and was ashamed of things I had done in my past. I just wanted to get out of the restaurant and isolate myself somewhere.

My depression lasted for several days. I wanted to be by myself, since I didn't feel worthy of the people around me, and I felt they would be better off if I were out of the picture. In the course of the restaurant conversation, my wife stated that she'd basically hidden from me by reading magazines. This revelation really hurt me, because for the last ten years I thought I had become so much better.

I have learned tools to deal with so many PTSD symptoms, and I believed she had seen the progress. At this point I questioned my efforts to try to improve.

After several days I made four conclusions based on this episode. First, I will never stop trying to improve. Second, I need to continue finding tools to help me improve. Third, the PTSD demons will always be lurking in my life. Fourth, I need to be more open about my past. I concluded that thinking things out and trying to make something positive come from a negative experience must mean I'm making progress. Previously, that depression would have lasted at least two weeks.

I learned that if I'm not totally open about myself and the terrible things I've done since returning from Vietnam, how can I continue to improve? This episode turned out to be a blessing in disguise. As I contemplated opening up about my post-Nam behavior, I realized that personal disclosure is a tool to recovery. I have experienced too much success, and my life has become so much better that I don't want to stop now. My demons will, from time to time, confront me. The next day after the event at the restaurant, I knew I was in trouble and called my buddy for help. He was there for me and talked me through my initial depression. Thanks to him, I didn't let the depression get out of control. He also suggested that I immediately write about it. In so doing I felt a lot better about myself. The following week I attended our PTSD meeting. The group consists of around ten veterans, who meet every two weeks. I brought up the story of my recent depression. I had intended to warn the others not to get themselves into the same situation I had. My brothers didn't see the issue the same way. They know my wife and respect her very much. Several of them pointed out that she had probably felt comfortable enough to vent openly about how my PTSD had affected her and the family. Of course, they were right, but while I was feeling sorry for myself, I hadn't realized that my actions or lack of actions had affected others.

This experience has provided me with another tool I can use to fight my PTSD symptoms. In retrospect I can now identify a large number of times I have reacted that way. When you're depressed, you tend to think of yourself and of how tough the world is on you. Unlike being backed into a corner or being hit cold with something, we have time to think in a situation like I experienced. If you have time to think, then you have time to make good choices. The tool I added was, "Consider those around you and the impact your behavior will have on them." I thank my buddy and the brothers in my group for speaking out. I also give myself some credit for listening and applying the tools I had learned. I would have had no idea how wrong I had been and never would have added this new tool to my toolbox. I hope by sharing this incident I will give other PTSD sufferers a better understanding of what we all are confronted with. The enemy we fight is PTSD, and he is smart, aggressive, and well equipped—and he holds the high ground. Don't allow yourself to be fooled into thinking the road to recovery is easy, and above all remember this: this enemy will always leave snipers behind to harass you.

When you're triggered, what's essential is first thinking about buying time. Just stop! Think out the situation—not only how the situation affects you. Delay saying anything and don't react until you consider how what you want to do or say would affect those around you. The tool of my buddy, LT— "It's not their fault"—is invaluable in this situation. We tend to be selfish and think of ourselves when we're triggered, thus forgetting it's our problem. In many cases we contribute to the situation, and in many cases we create the situation. Sometimes the problem is the fault of others, but don't jump to conclusions; think it out. If it's totally their fault, don't confront and don't fight. Your objective now is to remove yourself from the person, persons, or situation. If that isn't possible, like my restaurant episode, submitting may be best for all concerned. I'm a little hypocritical, since submission is as difficult for me as it may be for you. Whatever you do, avoid confrontation and fighting. Remember, we fight to win either physically as we were trained or orally using cruel, degrading, and harsh speech. Some things we say or do are difficult for others to forget or forgive.

CHAPTER TEN
Soldier in the Mirror:
Looking at Myself

One morning in my VA PTSD group, the facilitator asked what she had thought was a simple question: "What were you like before entering the military and going to Vietnam?" I became frustrated with trying to remember or identify what I had really been like. I remembered things I had done, but to describe what I was *like* seemed impossible. I knew what activities I had enjoyed, I knew the people I had liked to be around, and I knew the settings that had made me comfortable or happy. When she asked what I had been *like*, the question really meant, "How did others see you?" I think I was a likable person. I think others liked to be around me. I felt that most people viewed me as being respectful, a good friend, and a person with a strong value system. Unfortunately, after returning from Vietnam, I couldn't relate to that image of myself. The person I'd become wasn't the young civilian who'd enlisted several years earlier. For decades I lived with that new person, and I couldn't say that I particularly liked him. My recovery from PTSD involved my trying to create the person I would like to become. I wanted some of those lost characteristics I'd possessed before joining the military.

What had I been like? I know now that to help myself, I must be totally open and honest about my behavior upon my return from Vietnam. In a greater sense, maybe I should be more open about what I did or felt *in* Vietnam. If opening up about my behaviors when I returned is helpful, then why wouldn't it be helpful to open up about what I had done while I was there? I haven't gotten to that point yet, and it may or may not ever come to pass. I'm ready to face and share my adverse behaviors that happened after I got home, but what I did *in* Vietnam? I'm reluctant to open that Pandora's box.

I've been trying to recall the incidents in which I've exhibited my worst PTSD symptoms. I actually thought doing so would be simple. On the contrary, the task has been very difficult. The details are vague like so many details of what happened in Vietnam. I recall bits and pieces, some in great detail, but others remain very much a mystery. I apologize that I can't paint a more complete picture. If I tried this, I would be augmenting a memory or creating a memory that possibly wouldn't be true. Those who were around me are more accurate reporters of my actions. When I applied for PTSD compensation, I asked my wife, her sister, my ex-wife, and the buddy I had come home with to write letters on my behalf. The results were shocking to me but will probably give a better idea of what I was really like to live with and be around. Before I introduce those letters, I will tell you what I do recall.

I carefully guarded everything in my perimeter. This included not only things but also my family, especially my wife. I feared losing them to the degree that I smothered them. I had to be aware of everything she did and everyplace she went. In the end this behavior led to a divorce after nearly fifteen years. I coached Little League, which sounds good. The problem was, I couldn't accept a loss. I don't believe I showed bad sportsmanship, but I demanded excellence from the kids. I approached teaching much the same way; I demanded excellence from them also.

If something triggered me, I would erupt, generally by showing an outburst of anger, cursing, or encouraging a fight. At times I drove drunk with my family in the car. I purchased codeine over the counter in Canada and transported it home to use throughout the year. It was my intervention to help me fight the demons. I had only one service buddy, and we both had PTSD. Consequently, we enabled each other. From what my wife has said, I was mean to her and the kids when I was drunk. I wasn't physical, but my words hurt her and the children just as much. I didn't realize how my family and those around me feared me. These comments aren't very specific, but my recall isn't much better. The unfortunate thing is that I didn't think I was that bad. It wasn't until I read the letters to the VA that I saw how my life had impacted the lives of so many people, including the ones I loved most.

I caution you when you get to this point. The truth is hard to accept, and when it confronts you, be ready for a lot of guilt and likely a depression that will follow. Have your tools close and your buddies even closer. Facing this realization and the pain associated with it requires help. Unfortunately, it's a necessary process to go through.

Here comes the agonizing part for me. I have elected to share my very personal account of how I viewed my behaviors after returning from Vietnam and compared it to how my two wives and family members viewed me. I will start by submitting to you my stressor to the VA in support of my claim. It will become obvious that my family interpreted my behaviors very differently. To illustrate this, I share with you their letters to the VA in support of my claim.

My primary stressor reads as follows:

In the past three years I have become involved with the Vietnam Veterans of America and was made aware of post-traumatic stress disorder (PTSD). Through this association, I have recognized that I suffer and have suffered from many of the symptoms of PTSD. After separation from the military and two tours in Vietnam, I just wanted to lead a normal life. However, in my quest for normality, I put many things under the carpet and wouldn't address them as problems. The incident in Vietnam that I believe affected me the most was during the first two days of the Tet Offensive of 1968. I was stationed in a camp with the Third Marine Shore Party, the Gia Le combat base between Hue and Phu Bai. The first day of the Tet Offensive, my battalion's first flight arrived in-country to begin its deployment. Even though I had been detached to the Third for several months, I was immediately transferred back to my battalion. During this transition, I felt out of control and helpless. The NVA and Viet Cong were hitting us with rockets and mortars constantly. Our perimeter came under attack on a random basis. To make matters worse, I was short men, separated from my fire teams, guns, and gear. Being separated from my M60s and much of the gear made me feel more help-less than I have ever been in my life. I had zero control over the situation. I believe my PTSD symptoms can be tied to those events. I had never felt like that prior to that situation. Since the Tet Offensive and the Battle for Hue City, I have to feel in control of most situations in my life. When I'm in control, I seem to be OK.

When I'm not in control or am threatened
with losing control, my symptoms surface,
most of the time in a negative way. My PTSD
cost me a marriage, which ended in divorce,
and alcoholism. My job choices ensured that I
would be in control. I would become angry and
anxious when I couldn't control my surroundings. When alcohol threatened my second marriage, I elected to run and remove myself from
negative situations. The running replaced alcohol. I take antidepressant drugs and sleeping
medication prescribed by my family physician.
I didn't go to the VA as I wasn't aware that these
symptoms were PTSD related. I tend to blame
others and deny my own responsibility. Most of
the time I just get depressed and talk to no one.
I run within myself. I feel alone. No one cares
or would understand. At these times, I could
just run to a woods and die. I try to please but
never seem to do enough. I am paranoid that I
haven't gained the respect of others and consequently withdraw into myself.

While I completed my claim for PTSD, the
form requested two stressors. Vietnam veterans,
above all, realize how difficult that task was for
me after spending two tours there. *Control* was the
single word I chose to use to describe the many
stressors I experienced. I am no different from any
Nam vet; how could I identify just one or even two?
Some Vietnam veterans did experience what they

considered to be the single event that contributed to their PTSD. Unlike them, whether it was my job there or my military responsibilities, being in control of the situation or myself made me an angel in Nam and a monster when I returned home.

I shared with you my primary stressor, and now I want to share with you the impact it had not only on me but also on those I loved and wanted to be normal for. If you think my control hurt me, the following letters my family members wrote indicate the agony it had on them. My pain was unbelievable when I read these letters. These letters were sent to the VA to support my PTSD claim.

My ex-wife wrote the following:

I was Rick's wife; we married in 1968 and were married for 15 years when I filed for divorce. The behaviors he demonstrated in our relationship and with our three wonderful children were the catalyst of our unfortunate separation. Rick has a good heart, but his instability and personality were destructive to our marriage. Some examples of this:

* Rick was extremely jealous and paranoid throughout our marriage. He would not trust me to go to the grocery by myself and prohibited me from working. He was suspicious of my activities although I gave him no reason to doubt my trust.

* He fought depression and was very up and down. The "downs" led to excessive alcohol

abusé that affected our children. The kids witnessed these unfortunate situations where the
alcohol indulgence was acted out in front of
them. This continued for years even after our
divorce.

* In addition to being alcoholic, Rick was
addicted to over-the-counter medications. He
would take a bottle of NyQuill almost every evening. I don't know for sure, but I think he was
hiding alcohol from me when we were married.

* Rick is extremely obsessive and controlling. He would not allow me to manage any
functions of the home including budgeting. I
was not allowed to get mail from the mailbox
throughout our marriage. When he can't be in
control, he withdraws and displays a martyred
persona. The controlling behavior manifested
itself in having to be the "winner," even in
trivial events. He had to win. I know that one
of our children had to have numerous hours
of psychological counseling to overcome the
problems Rick created.

* Rick has always had sleep disorders. He
would dream about Vietnam, and if you were
to approach the bed while he was sleeping, he
was delusional and would come at you like you
were the enemy. The kids and I would not go
near him while he was sleeping as he has been
violent and tried to hit us. He would only sleep
in short bits while watching movies to put him
to sleep.

I hope Rick gets the help he needs to lead a normal life. Although I am not with him, I know the kids would appreciate a father who doesn't exhibit some of these behaviors and mends their relationship. Rick now acknowledges the problems; however, the scars left from years of this treatment will take some time to heal. Please let me know if I can be of further assistance. I have years of this type of interaction with Rick. Unfortunately, this letter addresses only some of the pain he caused.

My current wife wrote the following:

I am writing to explain some of the symptoms of PTSD that I have observed in my husband, Richard A. Price. I have been married to Rick for 18 years (1988). Between the two of us we have six children ranging in age from 41 to 17 years.

When Rick and I were married, he was experiencing frequent nightmares. Although I was not able to decipher precisely what the nightmares were about, he would often lash out, striking me or fighting off some unknown assailant. He would then be frequently depressed for several days following, but was unable to talk about what was bothering him. Although these nightmares have decreased in frequency over the years, they continue to haunt him approximately one time a month.

Even today, however, Rick continues to have difficulty sleeping, generally falling asleep with the TV on, as he becomes quite restless when attempting to sleep without noise. Rick generally sleeps only 3-4 hours a night. Everyone in the household knows not to wake him, as his first reaction is usually to strike out. I have been hit several times unintentionally when I have bumped him in bed in the morning.

Rick struggled with alcohol abuse for many years of our marriage. He did not view himself as an alcoholic as he did not "need" alcohol every day. I feel strongly that although he was not "addicted" to alcohol, he was unable to control his consumption. If he had one drink, it always led to him becoming drunk and generally verbally abusive to our children and myself. He occasionally became physically violent and we separated on two occasions due to his alcohol abuse. Today, he does not partake of any alcoholic beverages, for which I am thankful.

In the early years of our marriage, Rick controlled most aspects of our lives. He maintained our finances, giving me an allowance each week. Although I rarely left the house without Rick, he would become quite upset if I returned home more than five minutes later than my estimated time of arrival, and this would frequently result in accusations of lying, cheating, or dishonesty. He was jealous of any conversation I had with men or individuals he

did not know. Today, Rick is not as controlling with my life, but he continues to require
a great deal of control of his day. He much
prefers routine and becomes anxious and irri-
table if a spontaneous change in plans occurs.
He is very protective of his personal property
and becomes upset if anything in his personal
space (i.e., his desk, his trunk, his work area) is
out of place or if items are not returned to the
precise spot.

Although Rick is a very loving husband and
father, he prefers to engage in quiet conversation or small group interactions. He does not
like crowded spaces or large loud gatherings.
Ours was not the house where kids hung out,
as the chaos that generally accompanies children's play would make Rick nervous and upset. He has very limited tolerance to horseplay
unless he is the one initiating it, and it stops
when he stops. When we go out to eat, he always sits with his back to the wall and prefers
to sit in corners where he has full view of the
room.

These are some of the behaviors I have
observed that I feel are related to Rick's experiences in Vietnam. As stated above, he is a loving
and caring husband and father. He continues
to work on being more relaxed in his expectations of others and his vigilance in monitoring
his personal space. It has taken a great deal of
work on his part (and some patience on the

part of his family) to get to where he is today, but his schedule and approach to others continues to be greatly affected by his need for control and order.

Thank you for consideration of this matter and for any assistance that you can provide my husband.

I was going to stop here but decided that if I was going to really point out how I have affected others, I needed to include the letter my sister-in-law submitted to the VA as well. She and her husband are retired psych nurses at a large VA hospital that worked with PTSD patients.

This letter is written at the request of Richard Price, my brother-in-law, to document behaviors that I have observed that may be related to the time he spent in Vietnam. I have known Rick since August 1988 when he started dating my sister. Since they have been married, I have witnessed the following behaviors that have caused concerns for his and her safety and in some cases required intervention:

Controlling behavior—Setting strict daily schedules and seemingly unforgiving of any fluctuations regardless of the reason. Limiting access to my sister for family members, permission for visits, she could not/would not visit us without Rick or his limits usually. I have feared angering Rick or crossing his "invisible line" and no longer being able to see or talk to my sister because of his interference. Contact with my sister's family is generally superficial.

Alcohol use—1990—becoming intoxicated to the point that the children ask for my and my husband's assistance because of their fear for my sister. 1990—verbally challenging, then physically aggressive during a volleyball game requiring others to intervene. To my knowledge he has quit drinking for many years.

Anger management—Has very strict rules of conduct for others as well as himself and is very sensitive to offense if he feels the rules are not followed usually resulting in withdrawal and limited to no contact with the offender. Without the influence of alcohol, I have not noticed any physical violence in response to anger. I have witnessed verbally demeaning language toward his wife.

As a nurse in psychiatry for 30 years at a Cleveland VA and a concerned sister, I have at one time or another expressed all of the above concerns/issues with both my sister and my brother-in law. I do not know if any of Rick's behavior is related to PTSD. I do know that he has expressed acknowledgement of past problematic behaviors recently as the request for this letter indicates. My hope for Rick is to complete the healing process so he can fully enjoy the wonderful gifts he has in his wife, children, and family.

CHAPTER ELEVEN

Weapons in the Armory:
Tools to Fight PTSD

The conditioning I went through during my boot, ITR, and battalion military training was necessary for survival. Once it was applied for almost two years in Vietnam, the conditioning became my habits. Good or bad, habits are many, many more times harder to break than they are to form. That a great deal of reconditioning would be necessary to break those habits learned in training and applied in combat only makes sense.

Such a reconditioning never took place, and the habits were allowed to remain part of my life for decades. PTSD symptoms became a part of me. Those around me couldn't distinguish my habits from me. PTSD manifested itself as a part of my being and was reinforced by festering over time. Consequently, for many years I remained in my fantasy world. I thought I was OK and that the rest of the world was messed up. Later I recognized that I had problems but didn't know what to do or where to go for help. Through my buddies, I was able to gather tools that actually helped. I want to share the tools that have worked for me and a number of my Vietnam buddies. There are different tools for different jobs. I can't select tools without knowing the job I've been ask to work on. PTSD is this way; you can't work on it until you determine how you're affected.

When PTSD is recognized by the veteran suffering from it, it generally isn't recognized for what it is. The previous paragraph somewhat explains why. Veterans in this category continue exhibiting PTSD symptoms but actually believe the symptoms are part of their character, habits, and values; and in some cases they are. Those who accept PTSD without even recognizing what it is will continue through life accepting the person they are.

Other Vietnam veterans recognize something is wrong but have no idea how to fix it. Recognition that problems exist may come at any time following departure from Vietnam. Generally, what we identify as problems doesn't occur immediately, but signs may start to surface, as it did with me. Usually it takes one gigantic event (usually negative) or a series of repeated events (also negative) for the veteran to realize something isn't quite right.

Now you may say, "Fine. Let's fix the problem or problems." It isn't that easy! Recognizing that you have a problem doesn't ensure that you can come up with a solution. Remember, we have isolated ourselves for the most part. We exercise physical isolation as well as communicative isolation. We don't want to share our problems with those who don't understand, and most people are uncomfortable or fear approaching us about our problems. So we need help, and we recognize we need help, but we have no idea where to seek it. In some cases we aren't even aware that Vietnam and PTSD are the roots of our problems.

Like so many Vietnam veterans, I knew I had problems but wasn't aware of their origin. Consequently, if things got really bad and I ended up in a self-destructive depression, I would seek out a random psychiatrist, psychologist, or therapist. This approach was ineffective since I had no idea where the problems had originated. I couldn't help the medical professionals with this, and God knows they didn't help me. At the demand of my wife, I gave up alcohol as a form of intervention, since I was approaching the loss of a second marriage.

I sought help from several medical doctors, each experimenting with antidepressants. The medications seemed to help some, but the primary problems weren't being addressed. In desperation I went back to my last doctor and requested an antianxiety medication. He put me on a medication that would last about four hours before the problems came back. It was at this time that I realized I could purchase a low-dose codeine in Canada.

We went to Canada on vacation each year, and I would stock up on bottles of codeine, which lasted all winter. It wasn't uncommon for me to take four pills a day along with my other drugs. This routine went on for a number of years until I was able to get the real help I needed. During that entire time, I wasn't addressing the cause. Hell, I didn't know what the cause was. I was naïve enough to think flashbacks and nightmares were common to combat veterans, and I dismissed that they were connected to my mental status.

It wasn't until I retired and moved back home that I started to get more involved with the local veteran organizations. I felt comfortable with some of these brothers and began opening up a bit. Mainly I listened to them. I spent the first several years gaining trust and sharing incidental stories. On occasion a serious discussion would take place. It occurred when a select group of boots-on-the-ground veterans happened to be together. The discussion happened only when the group consisted of veterans who had gained trust in each other. It was during these times that I became more and more aware that we shared a lot of common life issues, problems, and experiences. One of my buddies in our group of veteran friends pointed out that I had symptoms of PTSD and asked me to read a booklet published by the Order of the Purple Heart. The booklet summarized the symptoms of PTSD. Upon reading the booklet, I realized I had most of the symptoms, and most importantly, *I wasn't alone.*

Without the association with my fellow veterans, I would never have recognized the root of my problems. I firmly believe affiliating ourselves with those who experienced similar combat situations is necessary. While veteran's problems are not exactly alike or perceived the same way, there is enough similarity that we can relate to each other. This is the first step to returning home and hopefully experiencing a somewhat normal life.

The next step in coping with the demons of PTSD is to identify ourselves with the tools or weapons that allow us to fight them and the symptoms they so graciously share with us. Having the VA prescribe medications to allow us to buy time to access more tools may be necessary. Tools that are most effective come from fellow veterans. The tools veterans develop are tools that have been tried in the trenches and found to work. Who better knows what will or will not work than a brother who has been there? Therefore, associating ourselves with fellow veterans who recognize they also need help is critical. Most importantly, make sure these veterans not only recognize they need help but also are willing to work at it. Working with these brothers will not only help us but also help them. The benefits gained from these comradeships are immeasurable.

It's during this step that we start to realize there is a great amount of satisfaction in helping each other, particularly if it involves a veteran who isn't as far along as we are. Every time a tool is shared that works for us, that tool may enhance the life of a fellow Vietnam veteran.

I would like to say that the small group I'm involved with happened by design, but it didn't! The group just evolved out of trust and need. We were fortunate that it evolved into a tool in itself. Most of us who gather at our Veterans Service Office twice a month look forward to the meeting and feel bad if, for some reason, it's canceled or we have to miss a meeting. Our meeting started out as a microsocial gathering, in which we could talk in comfort and trust. Occasionally, a topic would be introduced that one or more of us really related to. This would evolve into telephone or personal conversations about the issue. Our social meetings became quite regular, and since what we talked about became more and more Vietnam issue related, we decided to form our own PTSD group. The whole process probably took two years, but it was worth it. Now we welcome new veterans from current wars and new Vietnam veterans as well. Our group concentrates on getting better and finding tools to help in the process. Those who come for other reasons don't generally become a regular fixture.

The semistructure of our meetings is always subject to change based on the needs of the members of the group. We start by checking the status of every veteran present and carefully attend to his responses to ensure that he is indeed OK. If one of the group members is having a problem, we listen and attempt to offer help if doing so is within our scope. Several times we have recommended and assisted a member in getting help we couldn't provide. Help needs to be immediate. Unlike many who profess to need help, a veteran in need can't wait until Monday or after the holidays. When you need help, you need it now. If we can offer suggestions or give ideas on tools that may help, we do so. Sometimes we introduce and discuss tools we found that have helped us. Other times we spend the entire evening talking about the activities going on in our lives, our hobbies, or our interests. These are also tools some veterans need (comradeship). If conversation slows (which is rare), questions, comments, or veteran-related information is shared.

Meetings may be two hours in length, but many times topics from the meeting spill into the hall or parking lot. This tendency indicates that a particular topic held deeper meaning to several veterans. This may be a situation that sets the stage for one-on-one veteran pairing.

One-on-one pairing isn't planned but seems to evolve out of some form of inner connection between veterans. It can include more than two individuals, but two seem to work extremely well. There could be many reasons why the bonding takes place. For the purpose of being there to help each other, the reasons need not be identified. If you recall, in the Nam there was one buddy you had a special bond with. He was important then, and he's important now! The importance now is having the buddy available when you need him and your availability when he needs you. Your buddy is a top-priority commitment. Being there for each other day or night is essential. As we all know too well, demons don't sleep or take vacations. In dealing with the demons, appropriate intervention has to occur ASAP. What better intervention could you want than a buddy who's got your back?

The number-one goal in our small group is to assist in making life better for ourselves, spouses, family, and friends. In this attempt we have exchanged tools each has discovered works for himself. These tools are shared and discussed, not as a textbook presentation but rather through explanation by the veteran who found the tool to actually work. What is essential, when trying to implement a tool that has been discussed, is to practice it a number of times before concluding that it doesn't work for you. As the tool becomes more comfortable, you may decide to include it as a weapon to fight the demons.

A perfect example of this is my buddy's tool, "It's not their fault." At first I couldn't imagine *not* blaming others for actions I found upsetting. But I tried the tool a number of times and found that it did actually work for me. It bought me the time needed to think before I reacted. Even when I concluded the person or persons *were* to blame, I gained time to evaluate the situation. In doing so I was able to make more rational decisions on how to approach the situation.

As we all know, the feelings of anxiety and the loneliness of depression can be devastating. The tool I found to be most helpful is the Holy Bible. I have found that when I can't fight the demons alone or get a hold of a buddy, I can open the Bible to any page and within a few verses find some solitude. I'm no more a minister than I am a psychologist, but I am a Christian who believes the Holy Word of God is contained in the Bible. The New Testament (the Gospels) seems to give comfort more quickly. When using the Bible as a tool, go to the Gospels first. Answers and comfort can be found in the Old Testament as well. However, the answers are a little more abstract and difficult to extract quickly. In any case once you open the Bible, you will cease to be alone, and your thoughts will become more positive through the grace of God.

Help! Actually it should be stated, "Help others." While this may not sound like a tool that would help you with PTSD, it does. I was reluctant to start this topic, because I didn't know where to begin. As irony played out, my buddy had left a message on my cell phone to give him a call. This usually meant that something had triggered him, and he feared sliding into depression. I called him back to find that my suspicions were correct. We talked for a while, and during the conversation he was able to identify the initial event that had triggered him. Initial triggers are frequently difficult to identify, and many times a buddy can help you recognize them. As the result of our conversation, he felt much better and was able to avoid going into depression. My compensation was the wonderful feeling I had knowing that I had helped him. The feeling may also have come from the fact that it gave me self-worth. The more frequently you can provide help in this way, the better you will feel about yourself. A side benefit is that when you help others identify their triggers, identifying your own becomes easier.

I have a definite hierarchy related to the rewarding feelings I get from helping others. As a Vietnam veteran, Vietnam vets fall at the top of my list. I suspect that this partially comes from the lack of help we received upon our return from Vietnam. I'm sure our brotherhood plays an important role in my prioritizing as well. The respect I have for all veterans and their willingness to serve place them in a solid second along with my family. I am especially rewarded to help children and those older than I. This help gives me that sense of self-worth and value. Upon returning from Vietnam, I was deprived of most of these emotions. Finding a way to get them back is definitely a tool that helps fight the demons of PTSD.

As with most things, there is a downside to the "helping others" tool. We put ourselves out there. Just as we did in Vietnam, we are doing it again. Each time we attempt to help others, this effort makes us vulnerable and potentially in a defenseless position. Speaking for one who has experienced setbacks from the "helping others" tool, veterans need to keep aware of two possibilities. In the pursuit to help, we encounter users and/or manipulators. Unfortunately, these types of people exist in any group including Vietnam veterans and veterans in general. What I find most painful is when a Vietnam brother happens to fall into these categories. When we realize we're dealing with someone like this, trust is shattered and can set off a primary trigger leading to a PTSD depression. I differentiate between depression and PTSD depression in that PTSD depression involves being affected by the many variables we are trying to deal with—trust, self-worth, and value, to mention a few.

When using the "helping others" tool as a means to become stronger yourself, you must be cautious of overextending yourself. Your helpful contributions can also develop into a demon. When you overextend yourself in being helpful or involved, you can easily become less effective and start resenting the sacrifices made in an effort to be helpful. Remember, our goal is to turn our lives with PTSD into something *more* normal. This goal includes our relationships with family and friends. We have neglected them too long, and neglecting them now is not progress for us but rather another setback.

Another tool that can get us into a similar situation is our involvement in veteran activities. Once we get involved in an activity or organization, our natural military tendency is to give 100 percent. Because we were workaholics and sometimes alcoholics, slipping into a mode of being a "helpaholic" is easy. In so doing we frequently forget others and other meaningful activities we should be attending to. What becomes tough is that when we start to back off from a helpful commitment, we feel guilty. A veteran suffering from PTSD should try to avoid feeling guilty at all cost. The bottom line is, beware of overextending yourself in the beginning. Discuss your involvement in activities with your family. Check your other commitments before volunteering for something new. It's not like a firefight where it's all instant reaction—you *can* and *should* take the time to consider the impact helping or becoming involved has on your life and on the lives of your loved ones.

This situation is very similar to your reaction to a trigger. As you need to buy time to make better choices when triggered, you need to buy time to make good choices on commitments.

A tool that is necessary for me is my ongoing need to associate with Vietnam veteran brothers or veteran groups. I need the comradeship of my fellow Vietnam veterans. If you should elect to single out just one buddy, I need to caution you about a trap Grimshaw and I fell into. My brother, whom I dedicated this book to, was with me during most of my two tours in Vietnam. We both suffered from PTSD but weren't aware of it. We were close incountry and remained close after returning home.

Biological brothers couldn't have been closer. Neither of us really involved ourselves with other Vietnam veterans. As a result, we enabled each other's PTSD symptoms. All this managed to do was delay my acknowledging that I had PTSD, and he never acknowledged it. It was so easy! We had learned to trust and rely on each other all the time in-country. Our trust and reliance in each other were so strong that we never found a need for other opinions. We supported each other through divorces, alcoholism, raising children, and many other decisions affecting our lives and the lives of those around us. I can tell you that without the Vietnam brothers I have today, I would still be in the pit with my demons.

No one understands us like one of our own. When we returned home, no one understood us, and for that matter no one seemed to want to. As a result we felt isolated, or we isolated ourselves. Simply being around brothers who understand allows us to feel the companionship we desired having for so many years.

As I neared the end of this chapter, I realized my toolbox didn't seem very full, so I tried to identify other tools that might be helpful to anyone suffering from PTSD symptoms. I jotted down a few and was going to try to explain their potential benefits. It was then that I recognized that the tools I have already talked about were the only actual tools I have used and that worked for me. An additional list would only be recommendations. While they may sound good, I can't verify that they would work any better for me than for my fellow Vietnam veterans. I also realized they were becoming more general in nature and somewhat less typical of just Vietnam veterans.

The attempt to identify additional tools led me to an eye-opening revelation. As my tool list developed, I realized that what I was listing were intrinsic parts of me and my value system. Unlike the beneficial tools I previously identified, the extended list of tools was intangible; rather, they were a collection of deep-seated convictions and beliefs that were part of my being. This realization was both alarming and gratifying at the same time. I was alarmed that I hadn't recognized my own transformation while writing this book. All of a sudden I was confronted with the many realizations I had discovered about myself—where I had come from and where I wanted to take myself. I was even more alarmed to realize that I was nearly where I wanted to be. While I was alarmed that it had come to me all at once, I was gratified in that I was beginning to be able to live with myself and, in so doing, make it easier for others to live with me. In the early pages of this book, I listed what I thought would make me normal in my eyes and in the eyes of society. I suspect that in the many hours of soul searching, writing, and rewriting, I had not only identified the demons but also acquired knowledge of the weapons needed to keep them at bay or defeat them. Somewhere forty-plus years ago and in the decades that followed, I lost touch with the truth of normality. Under the cloak of war and combat, the elements of normalcy were lost. When I left Vietnam, I thought being normal was a collection of goals I needed to achieve. I couldn't have been more wrong.

CHAPTER TWELVE
Discharge from Active Duty:
My Conclusion

Throughout this book you have been exposed to one veteran's quest for normalcy. Most readers will probably expect that I found closure after the forty-four-year journey. On the contrary you have traveled through the years with me toward a destination that's impossible to reach.

I have discovered there is no cure for PTSD. However, with positive intervention, help from fellow vets, gut-wrenching dedication to becoming better, and above all, opening my heart to God, I can more easily cope and modify many of the demons Vietnam and PTSD made part of my life for so many years. With the grace of God, I have managed to turn many of them into an almost-positive part of my life.

During my writing I encountered writer's block a number of times, since some sections were difficult to face and much more difficult to express.

Difficult as the writing was, I've remained faithful to my goal and focused on my life and on the many ups and downs I've experienced after stepping off the casket-laden cargo flight at Travis Air Force Base in 1968. All I wanted was to find a normal life and be accepted by society for who I was—a society and country I felt I had sacrificed for and believed in. That society wasn't ready for me and most Vietnam veterans returning home. As a result, many of us reverted back to behaviors that had been accepted in-country. These behaviors had been learned during boot camps and honed to a fine art in the jungles, fire bases, and operations in Vietnam. We brought these behaviors home and, lacking societal support, made them the foundation of our "normal" lives.

In the Author's note you may recall that my purpose in writing this book was to help other Vietnam veterans. In the end I am the beneficiary of my own efforts. I discovered two things. First, I discovered how much depth I could go into about Vietnam and the personal aftermath of those experiences. Second and most importantly, I now know what normal really is.

Writing about my life after Vietnam was difficult enough. If I were to write about my two tours there, the document could be only about humorous incidents and funny stories. These I recall vividly, since they were all we had to keep ourselves sane in an insane place. Verbalizing my combat and the hideous things associated with it wouldn't benefit anyone, least of all myself. I have managed to tuck the details of those experiences away somewhere in the depths of my mind. The main incidents I recall, but the details only surface as dreams or unsolicited triggers. I could never imagine writing about those details, even if I could remember them accurately. I can describe the situation like this. It's like reading a book and remembering the title, introduction, and chapter headings. The remainder of the book is sketchy or forgotten. I believe that is why the dreams and triggers have such a devastating effect on me.

As I look back over my life since Vietnam, I realize I chained myself to a normal that was nothing more than a fairy tale, a fairy tale imagined by a young man who had matured at an abnormal rate. While I remained adolescent in many ways, my maturity had evolved to that of an old man. All things are accelerated in a war zone, so why would my conception of maturity be any different? I would offer that even boredom is accelerated. I would conclude that Vietnam had two speeds, exceedingly fast or painfully slow. The boring times allowed a young man's thoughts and dreams to become realities and goals in his mind. Contributing factors included fighting a war ten thousand miles from home, being separated from loved ones, desiring the life I had left behind, being deprived of developing at a normal rate, and, most of all, having to live in an insane environment.

Each section in this book exposed the myths of what I had considered normal to me forty-four years ago. I now realize that normal is a nominal set of values society expects from its members. Normal is fluid and in a constant state of change. One can deviate a little either way and still fall in the realm of societal acceptance as "normal." Vietnam veterans frequently exceeded those tolerances, and society's reaction was to pretend the Vietnam War and the soldiers who had fought it would just disappear. Hopefully society will someday understand, accept, and acknowledge the Vietnam veteran.

Welcome home, brothers. God bless us and our loved ones, whose lives were made hell by our sacrifice.

Biography

Richard Price enlisted in the US Navy Seabees in 1966 at the age of twenty-two as a surveyor. He served two tours in Vietnam and was attached to the Third Marine Shore Party at the Gia Le combat base during the Battle for Hue City in the 1968 Tet Offensive. After his military service, Richard became a vocational teacher of drafting and surveying. He went on to pursue his PhD in education and became a professor at both The Ohio State University and Kent State University. He is now retired and lives with his wife, Patty, in Newark, Ohio. He is actively involved in multiple veteran organizations including the Vietnam Veterans of America, the Veterans of Foreign Wars, the American Legion, Disabled American Veterans, and Amvets. He has melded his educational interests with this military background by publishing a children's coloring book on patriotism and America's military history. Because of this book, the Buckeye State Council of Vietnam

Veterans of America awarded him 2013 Veteran of the Year. He and his wife are actively involved in support groups for veterans and their families struggling with PTSD.

34913161R00111

Made in the USA
Charleston, SC
22 October 2014